Winning the Math Wars

No Teacher Left Behind

Winning

the Math Wars

No Teacher Left Behind

MARTIN ABBOTT

DUANE BAKER

KAREN SMITH

THOMAS TRZYNA

Washington School Research Center • *Seattle*

in association with

University of Washington Press • *Seattle & London*

© 2010 by the Washington School Research Center
Printed in the United States of America
16 14 12 11 10   5 4 3 2 1

University of Washington Press
P.O. Box 50096, Seattle, WA 98145 U.S.A.
www.washington.edu/uwpress

Library of Congress Cataloging-in-Publication Data
Winning the math wars : no teacher left behind / Martin Abbott ... [et al.].
p. cm.
Includes bibliographical references and index.
ISBN 978-0-295-98967-9 (pbk. : alk. paper)
1. Mathematics—Study and teaching—Washington (State) 2. Mathematics
teachers—Training of—Washington (State) 3. Curriculum planning—
Washington (State) I. Abbott, Martin, 1949–
QA13.5.W2W56 2010   510.71'0797—dc22   2009032579

The paper used in this publication is acid-free and 90 percent recycled from
at least 50 percent post-consumer waste. It meets the minimum requirements
of American National Standard for Information Sciences—Permanence of
Paper for Printed Library Materials, ANSI Z39.48-1984. ∞

Contents

Preface

Winning the Math Wars is the product of intensive research into the math education debate in the State of Washington, the United States, and the world. Researchers at the Washington School Research Center (WSRC) reviewed the current literature, summarized their own research, conversed with experts who hold widely differing opinions about the issues, and explored the various curricula proposed for improving math education. In the end, we have reached our own tentative conclusions about the additional empirical research needed into the teaching of mathematics. We also reached a conclusion about the extent to which math reform has been implemented in the United States and the places where support and new policies may be helpful.

Readers will not find a strong argument either in favor of traditional math education or in favor of a complete transformation of math education. We do believe that the debate over curricula, whether traditionalist, reform-based or constructivist, or ethnomathematical, must take second place to a discussion about the kinds of support and education that math teachers need in order to present any curriculum more effectively.

Abbreviations Used in the Text

ACME   Advisory Committee on Mathematics Education (UK)
AYP   Adequate Yearly Progress
CGI   Cognitively guided instruction
EALRs   Essential Academic Learning Requirements
EWU   Eastern Washington University
FIMS   First International Mathematics Study
GLE   Grade level expectation
IAEEA   International Association for the Evaluation of Educational Achievement
MEC   Mathematics Education Collaborative
MSP   Math-Science Partnership
NAEP   National Assessment of Educational Progress
NCATE   National Council for Accreditation of Teacher Education
NCES   National Center for Educational Statistics
NCLB   No Child Left Behind (Elementary and Secondary Education Act of 2002)
NCTM   National Council of Teachers of Mathematics
NMAP   National Math Advisory Panel
NRC   National Research Council
OECD   Organization for Economic Cooperation and Development
OSPI   Office of Superintendent of Public Instruction (Washington State)
PISA   Program for International Student Achievement
PLC   Professional learning community
PRiSSM Partnership for Reform in Secondary Science and Mathematics
RME   Realistic Mathematics Education (The Netherlands)
SIMS   Second International Mathematics Study
TAOP   Teaching Attributes Observation Protocol
TIMSS   Third International Mathematics and Science Study
UW   University of Washington
WACTE   Washington Association of Colleges for Teacher Education
WASL   Washington Assessment of Student Learning
WSRC   Washington School Research Center
WSU   Washington State University

Winning the Math Wars

No Teacher Left Behind

Introduction

A student remarked recently that high school geometry "was the most boring class I ever had in my life," despite the fact that he was very interested in math and science. As he looked back on his high school math classes, he realized that what he had chosen to study in college and beyond had been seriously, and negatively, conditioned by this high school experience. Now graduated from college, the student wondered how different his future might have been if he had learned math in a different way. "We memorized formulas and proofs; if the teacher had taken me outside and shown me that I could find the distance to an unknown point just knowing an angle, I would have been much more engaged with the question and understood geometry as a discovery possibility."

This is not an isolated comment; no doubt everyone reading this book has heard similar things about math classes. Whether or not a student learns geometry well is a function of many things, not the least of which, of course, is the extent to which he or she is engaged in the subject and the extent of his or her overall aptitude for learning.

It is important to point out, however, that the reasons for learning mathematics well often lie "outside" as well as "inside" the individual. Learning is related not only to the student's own motivation and capability, but also to the nature of teaching, the curriculum in use, features of the learning environment, district policies that affect math offerings, and so on. One could argue, for example (and it has been argued forcefully and repeatedly), that if the teacher were more interesting, the problem would be solved. But the same "inside/outside" dynamic applies. Whether or not the teacher is "more interesting" is a function of the teacher's own motivation as well as other factors: Is professional development relevant and timely? Do other math teachers regularly interact on lessons and about individual students? Do district policies ensure an adequate support system for mathematics instruction? Researchers, practitioners, educational leaders, parents, and policy makers all have suggestions about these and other factors and how they can be changed to positively impact student learning in math. Moreover, these individuals and groups can have very strident opinions that are often in conflict. Who is right and who is wrong?

One of the main premises of this book, consonant with much previous research, is that the teacher's role is critical. Teachers stand between the students, with their mixed readiness to learn, and the school system, which can be helpful or harmful to a teacher's efforts to provide meaningful learning experiences in the classroom. We therefore want to note the elements of current and proposed educational reforms that have the potential to leave math teachers behind. We hope to underscore the need for supporting teachers to do their best in what they are called upon to do.

Four Critical Insights

Over the course of our research, we identified several factors that seem to affect the nature of math education reform and student academic achievement. Our insights are not necessarily new, but they do suggest new directions for resolving the debates about how to improve math teaching and learning.

1. Fidelity

Reform efforts have not led to improved student outcomes because teachers have not been given the support necessary to change/align instruction with the standards-based system of education.

Our research suggests that tests of mathematical achievement do not tell us much about the value of reform efforts because these reforms have not been implemented fully. Reform efforts may be unsuccessful because teachers are not given the support necessary to change the way they teach or even to understand the mathematical and pedagogical ideas at the center of the reformed curricula. The most sophisticated and well-conceived reform effort imaginable may fail because the means of carrying it out are not in place. This is a two-fold problem. First, fidelity to reform efforts usually requires change in the approach to teaching and learning. Faced with a lack of appropriate resources and information, school leaders and teaching staff may revert to what they have always done rather than grapple with the new expectations. The second problem relates to support: Is the reform effort comprehensive? Changing one part of a system may be helpful, but if the entire system is not changed and aligned with reform principles, the partial effort is usually ineffective. To put the point baldly, you cannot point to test results to prove the success or failure of a particular textbook or approach to instruction, because what really happens behind the closed doors of many classrooms may not be what the reform efforts mandated.

2. Focus on Instruction

Effective reform requires coordination among three essential components: curriculum, instruction, and assessment.

Math reform is usually approached from the standpoints of curriculum/standards and assessment/accountability, leaving out instruction. It may be easier to adopt a new curriculum or devise a new assessment than require teaching itself to change in fundamental ways. Not that any of these is easy! Reform efforts can lose momentum in any of the three related components, but it is probably more difficult to completely revise the way teachers view their craft than to restructure the way a district organizes its learning protocol. Leaving out instruction means that no attention is paid to what teachers know about their subject or to the skills they need to communicate effectively to students. Instead, reformers have tended to assume that fresh approaches to instruction and enhanced abilities to understand and teach math would follow naturally once teachers were given the "right" curriculum and told that they would be held accountable by statewide tests. But this has not been true on a large scale or for most teachers and programs.

3. Mathematical Knowledge

Mathematics knowledge is essential to successful reform.

While high-quality curricula along with appropriate and effective assessments are necessary to improve math education, it is critical for teachers to know their math thoroughly and also to have well-honed abilities to convey mathematical ideas. Research suggests that many teachers in the elementary grades, where the real foundations of mathematical understanding are laid, do not know enough mathematics and in some cases are uncomfortable with math. Therefore, efforts to enhance the mathematical knowledge of teachers are highly important, as Stigler and Hiebert (1999) and others have argued for many years. However, it is not enough simply for teachers to know their math well, because as Ball, et al. (2007) and Ma (1999) have shown, teaching math well requires a specialized knowledge of techniques for communicating the abstractions of mathematical ideas. Researchers are only just beginning to understand what makes some math teachers truly great—how they talk about abstract ideas, how they respond to questions, how they deal with common errors of understanding, and how they use examples and a multiplicity of learning techniques to help students to make math their own.

4. Transformational Change

As the view of teachers toward their work and themselves changes, systematic and meaningful reform can occur and persist. But the educational institution must provide a supportive context that will not inhibit but rather will foster the "living out" of these changes in the classroom.

This fourth "dimension" of reform follows closely from the preceding three. Overall reform efforts require structural and organizational support for teachers once reform efforts begin ("fidelity"). This support enables teachers to adopt more efficient pedagogy rather than rely on changes to curricula and assessment alone ("focus on instruction"). But real change requires greater teacher knowledge of mathematics in combination with revitalized pedagogy ("mathematical knowledge"). Finally, at a fundamental level, educators must continually challenge the views they hold of themselves in their work with students, and the districts that support their work must continually re-evaluate their support systems for teaching and learning.

There are two components to transformational change: intra-individual change and institutional change. Both of these areas are best understood through examining the process of change in educational practice. The work in the WSRC on meaningful change in education has identified the importance of "first-order changes" (external components thought to lead to better student performance, such as smaller classes, having access to student data, etc.) leading to "second-order changes" (e.g., capitalizing on the use of smaller classes and student data to qualitatively change the learning experience for the student). That is, the first-order changes do not represent reform by themselves; true reform occurs when second-order changes emerge from the successful negotiation of the first-order assets.[1]

If transformational change is to occur, teachers of mathematics ("intra-individual change") must fundamentally change the way in which they interpret themselves vis-à-vis mathematical knowledge, specific lessons and/or curricula, and their goals for teaching mathematics. In the language of first- and second-order changes, they must undergo a second-order change in their understanding and practice of mathematics, building upon the advantages of the first-order changes that accrue from reform efforts.

The second component of transformational change is institutional support. If the intra-individual changes are not allowed to bloom within the institution of which the teacher is a part, the momentum and outcomes in math education will wither and die. This follows a very old sociological principle that points to the nature of the world "outside" the individual having a good deal to do with how the individual sees the world from the "inside." In the dynamic of changes to math education, we might say that even if teachers gain profound new views of themselves in their role as math teachers, they will revert to their old views unless institutional supports are in place to ensure that the teachers can "live out" and practice their new identity. If school administrators and other teachers have not changed their thinking, if the teachers are not provided appropriate professional development and time to consolidate their thinking with like-minded individuals, the "new thinking" will not gain a foothold.

---

1. See Fouts (April 2003) for the complete explanation of first- and second-order changes.

The Problem in Context

We have chosen to review the state of math education by looking at a wide swath of materials published by scholars and commentators throughout the world, the United States, and the state of Washington. Our primary conclusions mirror some of those published by such scholars as James Stigler at UCLA, Deborah Ball at the University of Michigan, and Liping Ma at Stanford University. As educational researchers and consultants, we have been active in math education, in educational assessment, and in policy development, and we bring that experience to this study. We have also entered into open and respectful conversations with experts who represent the principal, often opposing, and sometimes fiercely held, positions in the discussion. Across the world, advocates of traditional methods have crossed swords with partisans of a variety of new methods, from the New Math of the post-Sputnik years to the reform-based or constructivist mathematics of the present. Their debate over the best curricular designs and educational objectives has been further affected by the emergence of "ethnomathematics." Readers who are not familiar with these fascinating debates will find a historical review of these trends here.

We have also drawn on research by the WSRC on mathematics education and, more broadly, on all aspects of educational reform, not only in Washington State but in other parts of the United States. Our own conclusions do not necessarily affirm one curricular approach over another. Increasingly, we found ourselves focusing on the basic interaction between teacher and student, and like a number of major scholars in this field, we have been led to ask what we know about what happens when math is well taught. What goes on between student and teacher? What special knowledge of both math and the teaching of math does the teacher possess? Does the student learn something else, such as problem-solving skills, besides the answer to the math problem?

Plan of the Book

Our discussions therefore focus on the teacher, on "no teacher left behind," rather than on the virtues of any particular curriculum or the power of any testing regimen. We conclude with a call for additional research into the best methods for helping the present generation of math teachers to enhance their mathematical competencies. That work needs to be undergirded by studying the best practices of those teachers who understand how mathematics is learned and how to communicate with their students and point them toward success.

There is a glut of programs across the country attempting to change math education. But few educators understand the components of transformational change, i.e., that no matter how good the training, how innovative and clear the new curriculum, the teachers must fundamentally change the way they interpret mathematics, and the educational institution must accommodate the playing out of these new ways of doing business in the classroom. Many initiatives and programs will implement training and new curricula, but most will fail due to lack of attention to transformational change.

Our plan for this book is to consider the four principles we discussed above within the research and study of mathematics education on the international stage and across the United States. We include a study of the reform efforts in Washington State as an example of the processes we identify. Following these topics, we introduce several change efforts that contain the elements that might have a meaningful impact on math education generally. None of these is sufficient by itself, but each is a good example of what can be done at different stages of reform.

1

What the World Is Thinking

The international, American, and Washington State discussions of math education can be accurately described as microcosms of all the issues raised by the emergence of a global economy. Such discussions are driven by concerns about global economic and technological competition. The debates have a rich historical dimension that recalls the concerns of the Cold War, and they pit competing theories of education against one another. Just underneath the surface, these discussions reveal roots in ongoing analyses of how race, class, and colonialism have affected and continue to affect educational policy. Meanwhile, teachers around the world have been trying to convey complex mathematical ideas to generations of students while a debate rages around them and while being asked to modify their teaching practices according to one new curricular idea after another.

The world's math teachers are not doing so badly, all things considered. International surveys of math achievement are commonly used to show how nations rank and to level accusations, and yet careful study of those statistics indicates that most nations' overall performance is good. Every nation could do better, of course, and many nations would profit intellectually and economically if they were able to produce more graduates with baccalaureate or advanced degrees in math and engineering. If those improvements are to be achieved, what are the most important issues to address? Where can policy makers, teachers, educational administrators, parents, and other citizens make the most effective investment of time and public resources?

Concern about math education pre-dates Sputnik, although the Soviet Union's successful launch of a satellite, with the resulting crisis of confidence in the West, is generally considered a defining moment. The news media have continued since then to report falling math scores, new methods of teaching math have been introduced (and often scorned), and governments and foundations have commissioned numerous reports and systems of testing. Yet in spite of the often expressed conclusion that the world's system of education is in trouble, the pace of invention and technological innovation seems to increase rather than decrease.

A review of the world's discussion of math education therefore requires a framework of questions that can be used to sort and analyze what is being said. First, what is broken? Was there in the past some system for teaching math that has been lost because of unwise experimentation or some other deep cause? Second, what kind of mathematical knowledge, if any, is at risk? And third, what purposes are served by that mathematical knowledge? Why is math important? What is the value of a nation's ability to produce mathematicians?

Is the System Broken? (Or, Are We Falling Behind?)

Determining how to measure what is and is not working is the place to start. One such measure was implied by a recent newsletter published by the University of Michigan (Rho n.d.), which discussed the number of Americans who had won Fields and Abel medals, which are the equivalents of the Nobel Prize for mathematics. This kind of measure, in which America excels, shows the level of mathematical creativity. American universities are respected throughout the world for their excellence and their productivity, so the number of medalists may be an indicator of the continued creative and inventive abilities fostered in the relatively open environment of the American university, where students have more opportunities than elsewhere to explore, to change majors, and to learn through inquiry. This approach to measuring excellence is open to criticism as elitist, however. As later chapters will show, the U.S. mathematics teaching establishment has made a strong commitment to serving all students rather than to putting the emphasis on training a small elite.

Some demographic evidence indicates that America has in fact been working gradually to increase access to math and science. A 2007 report in *Science Daily*, for example, reports that in 1930, only 29% of Americans graduated from high school, and of those, 15% took classes in physics, a typical math-intensive discipline. By 1970, 77% graduated from high school, and of those, 22% took physics. Since 2000, the number of students taking physics has increased 31%. Are these statistics consistent with the view that there is a crisis in math and science education?

To the contrary, however, David Klein's paper on the history of American mathematics education includes a graph that shows enrollment in algebra dropping from 56.9% in the 1909–1910 school year to 24.8% in the 1954–1955 school year (Klein 2003, p. 6).

Observers cite other measures, such as the declining number of Americans who complete degrees in mathematics and the increasing proportion of foreign students completing doctoral degrees in math at U.S. universities. Do these findings indicate that the U.S. is not producing enough students trained in math at the secondary level? Or do such statistics indicate that American universities are attracting the brightest students from around the world, which helps maintain the quality of our own research and which also benefits U.S. students enrolled in those programs? As for the argument that fewer

Americans are completing degrees in math, a fair analysis would have to take into consideration the number of students with good mathematical and logical skills who have entered emerging fields such as computer science.

Another reasonable objection might be made to some Americans' concern that the United States is falling behind in math. Judgment as to which nations' citizens do best cannot be made simply in terms of numbers of degrees, or top scores on tests, or even comparisons of national average scores (which is the statistic most frequently cited in newspaper reports). Some nations excel when their top and average scores are compared, but the range of their students' scores is huge, indicating that many students are not well served by the national curricula and are truly left behind. The current American slogan for education, "no child left behind," translates into a national profile of test scores in which no child would have an extremely low score, but where the national average and the national highs may be a little lower than in those nations where there is more emphasis on differential placement of students and a greater willingness to leave some students behind.

The evidence for a crisis in math education is questionable on other grounds as well. Major international tests of mathematics competency compare very different kinds of students. As Iris Rotberg (1998) wrote of the 1995 Third International Mathematics and Science Study (TIMSS), "In Cyprus, students taking the advanced mathematics test were in their final year of the mathematics and science program; in France, the final year of the scientific track; in Lithuania, the final year of the mathematics and science gymnasia; in Sweden, the final year of the natural science or technology lines; and in Switzerland, the final year of the scientific track of the gymnasium" (p. 1030). Rotberg observed, finally, "In contrast, students in several countries, including the United States, attended comprehensive secondary schools. The major difference in student selectivity and school specialization across countries makes it virtually impossible to interpret the rankings" (Rotberg, n.d.). To summarize Rotberg's point, comparing a random sample of American high school students to Swedish students in selective science and math academies tells us nothing useful about the relative standing of American education. The fair comparison group for highly selective European gymnasia would be specialized math high schools in New York City, or the students of elite prep schools such as Phillips Exeter in New Hampshire or Lakeside in Seattle, Bill Gates' alma mater.

What Is at Risk?

The underlying concern appears to be a fear that America may find itself in a position where its economic and military dominance falters because the nation's schools and universities no longer produce an adequate number of geniuses to advance the economy and an adequate number of well-trained specialists to fill all the available positions in high-tech corporations and research centers. Reasoning of this kind leads to recommendations for tracking students early in order to achieve national expectations for numbers of degrees earned in specific areas of math and science. The latest British model of math education is returning to this kind of tracking, over the objections of some British education experts, such as the Advisory Committee on Mathematics Education (ACME) (2004). On the new UK model, which is perhaps a rebirth of previous UK tracking systems, students can choose to take a lower level math sequence that prepares them for blue collar work, or they can take a second and higher math track that readies them for advanced study and opportunities to pursue university degrees that have a high mathematical content. South Africa is another nation that has moved toward a kind of tracking that is driven by national assessment of the kind of "mathematical literacy" necessary for students to "contribute to modern life." The new lower math curriculum in South Africa focuses on what might be called business math, as reported by Sue Blaine in *Business Day* (June 2005).

The American system of higher education has differed from the European precisely in this detail, that the American system does not categorize students in such a final and irrevocable manner so early in life. The American model, while it may be inefficient, leaves open the possibility that students will bloom later, or may choose to work harder later. This debate over egalitarian versus highly selective or elitist education will probably grow more strident, particularly in Europe, where European Economic Community policies of open college enrollment are being reconsidered for two reasons. First, students are moving about the continent more freely, which creates difficulties for enrollment management, and second, many European nations are debating whether they can afford educational policies that allow less prepared students to take highly valuable places in university classrooms (Corbett 2005). This same debate between elitism and egalitarianism features prominently in the American discussion of mathematics education, especially since the National Council of Teachers of Mathematics (NCTM) made equality of access the top priority in its list of values for math education.

Categorizing students or tracking them into different levels of curricula seem at least partly rational at first glance. However, the problem with such tracking is that it is not clear what constitute the most basic skills that students should have to be able to function well in ordinary business settings. The most reductive approach to this question is to assure that all students have enough math to keep accounts. But other descriptions of basic math are possible if one takes into account new technologies and global business. Perhaps an understanding of interest rate calculations and foreign currency fluctuations are truly basic math. Perhaps, in a world where teenagers learn computer programming and dream of contributing to gaming, a knowledge of fractal geometry, quaternions, and Taylor series are basic math that may need to be taught in an order far different from the way they are traditionally introduced.

What Purposes Are Served?

As this and later chapters will explore, those who call themselves traditionalists in the math debate argue that the math that America needs is precisely the kind that allows students to do well in college calculus, differential equations, statistics, linear algebra, and the applications of those subjects. To the degree that current math education does not produce enough students with high skills in those areas, the nation has a problem. A professor at an Ivy League university published an argument to this effect, using as evidence the abilities demonstrated by his calculus students over a period of thirty years (Harper 2001). His students' performance had declined, from which he concluded that the teaching of math had deteriorated at the pre-college level, even for the best students. What our book explores is whether such a conclusion is justified, since the limited evidence available indicates that reform curricula, of whatever description, probably have not been adopted thoroughly in American classrooms. Moreover, our knowledge is limited concerning exactly how much American math teachers know about math and the teaching of math. To put this another way, we do not know how teachers' knowledge of mathematics and the teaching of mathematics has changed in the United States or elsewhere over the last thirty or fifty years.

One response to the concern about learning calculus has been a push to teach calculus in high school, a phenomenon that has grown over the past generation. Some constructivist scholars argue that it is a mistake to teach calculus in high school because colleges have done this very well and because there are more important basic reasoning skills that need to be mastered in high school and the lower grades (War-field 2007, Mallinson 2007). Throughout most of the world, including those nations that generally score higher on math tests than America, calculus is not viewed as the zenith of mathematics education. More time is spent on other matters, such as problem solving, statistics, and discrete mathematics. Hence the current NCTM guidelines suggest that more time ought to be spent teaching probability and statistics, which are in any case more useful than calculus to the average citizen for understanding public issues, and to those doing biomedical and social science research.

Even if we knew enough about math curricula and math teaching methods, it might still be true that the teaching methods that are letting some elite students down—in the sense that they don't achieve the same level of math ability as in previous generations—are the same methods that assure that the lower performers and those afraid of math are doing far better than their counterparts a generation ago. So in the end, the choice of a curriculum, which is an important social choice, may not depend solely on whether a nation wishes to keep up the supply of engineers and physicists. That choice also depends on how well a nation wishes to educate the majority of its citizens to understand new developments in science and technology. It has been observed that lower math scores on national tests may be due to a larger proportion of students having access to elementary, secondary, and tertiary higher education. But as later parts of this chapter demonstrate, it is difficult to form conclusions about such assertions.

And here another aspect of the issue emerges. School curricula and the informal curriculum of social learning now cover far more topics than in the past. Children in developed nations now commonly know basic computer programming and understand many technical details and have skills associated with digital cameras, video recorders, and advanced computer graphics systems. People are also exposed to highly technical information on television medical programs and through advertising for pharmaceuticals. In the face of this evidence that ordinary people are becoming more technically and scientifically literate, it is hard to believe that we are in the presence of an educational crisis.

How Do We Fix a Broken System (If It Is Broken)?

Whether the problem of math education is worldwide or American is an extremely complex question. The debate is complicated by disagreements over tests, bases of comparison, curricula, educational goals, underlying social and political goals, and many other factors. Whatever the positions taken by the participants in this debate, everyone who enters this contested territory wants mathematics to be understood better, more deeply, and more widely, applied more routinely, appreciated more universally, and approached with less fear of its being too difficult or too abstract for most people to understand and use. At the same time, there is little agreement about the answers to the questions posed at the beginning of this section. Was there a superior math curriculum in the past? Fifty or a hundred years ago, fewer students took advanced science and math, and technology was far simpler. What kind of mathematical knowledge is most important now? Americans aim for calculus, while much of the world places more emphasis on statistics and applied math. Our children may be more interested in shortcuts to learning the kinds of math that undergird computer graphics. What is the purpose of math education and should that purpose be the same for all segments of the population? Some would argue that the point is to maintain an economic, technological, and even military edge. Others see more value in assuring that everyone attains at least a competency sufficient to thrive in the business world.

Instead of asking about the reasons for the failure of math education, it may be helpful to ask, instead, how math education can be enhanced. What features of math education have been the subject of experiments? What, from an international perspective, is the full range of variables in the teaching of math? However, because the debate is framed so often in terms of problems and failures, it is easier to ask where the problem lies.

Where Does the Problem Lie?

In many nations, the results of international studies of math performance raise little public heat. The Japanese, for example, concluded that they ought to try harder to help students like math, in addition to mastering it (Macnab 2000). Some places, such as Hong Kong, have responded to the test results by adopting new curricula, abandoning traditional drills and tracking in order to serve more students who have been poor performers or who have shown math phobia (Lam n.d.). Perhaps in a generation it will be possible to look back and see if these changes have had any effect. Norway adopted a constructivist or new-new math curriculum and suffered a decline in national competency, though on close analysis it appeared that the curriculum was imposed without offering much training to teachers in how to use the methods (Bjorgqvist 2005). Above all, the United States and Britain have tried to find the reasons for lower mathematics performance as measured in major international tests that have been created and administered to a large degree by Anglo-American and Canadian experts. A quick review of the likely culprits for the perceived fall in achievement provides a context for understanding this debate—keeping in mind, of course, that those international tests may not provide comparable data at all.

Is the Real Problem American Culture?

Cultural and family educational values are often cited as important factors in math learning. Japanese parents drive their children to excel (Harper 2001). The Japanese educational system is designed to move pupils toward fearsome examinations that determine an individual's entire future. Students often go from long school sessions to afternoon and night cramming academies. Therefore, some experts argue there is little point in comparing Japanese (or Korean) education to US education, because it is not likely that America will adopt the parenting and schooling practices of these Asian nations. The studies by Rho (n.d.), Ellington (2005), and Harper (2001) address this question.

Is It a Time Issue?

Time on task is a second variable, as is evident already from the example of Japan. Records indicate that the amount of time spent in math classes has fallen in many nations as other subjects have been added to curricula. Moreover, time spent on math today is different from before, because the subject has broadened to include mapping, graphic presentation, and other topics that traditionalists consider outside the bounds of basic mathematical learning (i.e., the four principal operations of addition, subtraction, multiplication, and division, standard algorithms for those operations, elementary algebra, and geometry) (Ellington 2005, Harper 2001). There has also been pressure over recent decades to teach more math, sooner. Algebra has been pushed from ninth to eighth grade in many schools, and many high schools now offer calculus, a subject formerly taught primarily in the first year of college (Mallinson 2007). Obviously, these curricular choices are loaded with social and political values. The geographical knowledge communicated in studies of maps, for example, addresses a significant gap in American education. How might one choose between knowledge of geography and better knowledge of division?

Could the Problem Be the Mathematics Curriculum?

The scope of the curriculum is a third variable that is closely related to time on task. A common complaint about contemporary math curricula is that they are "a mile wide and an inch deep." Underlying this concern is a subtle argument that a lot of what is presented is not traditional math at all. Chapters on population geography that teach how to interpret charts and statistics are sometimes criticized on this ground. This concern about scope, however, touches implicitly on the question of teacher competence. Elementary teachers who do not have extensive training in math, or who are even afraid of math, may find this kind of curriculum a haven from teaching the basics, though conversely one might just as well say that such a curriculum offers a talented math teacher a rich chance to teach statistical concepts.

Those who study the scope of the math curriculum and time on task often use methods that are open to question. Asking a teacher to self-report the amount of time spent on new content compared to review of older material, for example, may have little meaning. New content often requires review of older material or reinforces older material. Combative reviews of textbooks written by partisans of one approach or the other commonly reduce an "enemy" textbook to a few stereotypes. One side claims that another's textbooks produce nothing but confusion; another side claims that the other's offers nothing but meaningless drill with no useful applications. The bibliography on these issues includes work by Raimi (2006), Ellis and Berry (2005), and Agarkar and Shirali (2001).

A more sophisticated critique of the tendency to include social science content in math textbooks is that students might be taught to take a fundamentally statistical approach to mathematical questions, an approach in which it is understood that math problems have no correct answers, only a plurality of possibilities for which arguments can be made on the basis of presentations of data through charts, tables, graphs, and even essays. Such an approach to truth is consistent with the notion that all values are socially constructed and that students should invent their own approaches to solving mathematical problems. This social constructivist or statistical approach to finding answers is a problem when, in fact, there are correct answers to well-defined questions. Of course, there is a difference between social constructivism and moral relativism on the one hand and constructivism as the term is used in education, where the intent is to emphasize the importance of students participating in problem solving by constructing answers rather than just memorizing methods. In a constructivist or reform-based curriculum, students come to understand through an internal process of grappling with problems and making sense of them.

Before proceeding to look at the competing models of math instruction in the world, it is helpful to examine a simple math problem to see the different kinds of answers that are so hotly contested. Consider the following problem. A farmer asks his two children to count the numbers of pigs and chickens in their yard. One child reports that there are 70 heads, the other that there are 200 feet. A standard algebraic solution to the problem is to recognize that the solution requires two equations with two variables, the number of pigs (P) and the number of chickens (C). In this standard approach, the two formulae are: P + C = 70 and P × (four legs per pig) + C × (two legs per chicken) = 200 legs. Substituting P = 70 − C into the second equation, you soon come to the conclusion that there must be 30 pigs, which have a total of 120 legs, and 40 chickens (which have a total of 80 legs). The algebraic method accomplishes two objectives: it produces an answer and it also implicitly demonstrates that there is only one answer.

A student who uses a guess and check approach to find an answer may get the same result, but guess and check will not show that there is only one answer to the problem because it does not frame the problem with the same kind of abstraction and generality. Using the guess and check method, a student might say, "I found only one answer to this problem," but statistically speaking, there may be five or six other and equally good answers. Of course, a student who just learns the rote method and creates two formulae out of habit may wonder in the end why that method worked and whether the answer actually makes sense. Therefore, a traditionalist may say that learning the algebraic method is the only approach to finding the correct answer, while a constructivist may say, with equal conviction, that guess and check or some other creative method may help a student think through the problem, with the result that the student actually develops better problem-solving skills and more confidence in the face of puzzles. The constructivist curriculum builds on what the student has learned by finding the answer any way he or she can, by then introducing algebraic approaches to solving the same problem. The ethnomathematical approach, which will be introduced later, adds another, political dimension to such a problem. And what if one of the chickens had two heads, or the children counted each other's heads and feet?

Are the Teachers the Problem?

Teacher preparation is a fourth important variable and, as we will discuss, perhaps the most important variable for American, if not world, education. In some nations, teachers must have completed two full years of college mathematics courses, the equivalent of a strong math major, to teach math at almost any level. The underlying logic of such a social choice appears to be that a teacher who is adept at working with math of all kinds is likely to be a creative and effective instructor of mathematical principles, even in first grade. The findings of this book, and one of our discussion points, is that while it may be important for math teachers to enjoy math and to know a great deal of math, there is a difference between knowing math and knowing how to teach math. More particularly, those who "get" math easily may not always be the best people to help students who need to be taught by instructors who recognize common errors of learning and who can provide support and alternative strategies for understanding the mathematics needed in any given context.

To return to the issue of basic preparation, American primary teachers, like their peers in many other nations, often have as few as nine college credits of math and math-teaching classes. Moreover, the school systems in which they teach may not provide the kind of in-service education that would help them learn the specific skills necessary for teaching math effectively. Whether the world has an adequate knowledge of those pedagogical skills is a question taken up at the end of this volume. Ole Bjorgqvist, writing of the success of Finnish math education, provides a picture of a complete system with all of its elements created for success. Finland is ethnically homogeneous. Teachers are well paid. All teachers must have extensive training and also complete a master's degree in pedagogy with a research thesis, and pre-service teacher training is extensive (Bjorgqvist, 2005). James Stigler and James Hiebert of UCLA say of the state of American math education, "our biggest problem is not how we teach but that we have no way of getting better" (Stigler and Hiebert 1997, p. 1). Stigler and Hiebert describe the vast network of American math teachers at all stages in their careers and ask what kind of interventions and research can be used to identify best practices and teaching knowledge and how to impart that knowledge across the nation to current and future teachers alike.

America is not alone in this discussion. Japanese and Chinese teachers participate in ongoing professional development activities aimed at improving basic knowledge of math and the effectiveness of daily math instruction (Ma 1999). In stark contrast, in some nations there are discussions about whether teachers should be required to complete even a bachelor's degree (Blanco 2003, Ding 2004).

Chinese math teachers focus on math instruction. When they are not teaching math, they are meeting with their peers to discuss methods for communicating content and problem-solving skills more effectively. In other nations, teachers at the primary level teach every subject. How can they be as adept at math instruction with such a diversity of teaching assignments and such broad expectations for knowledge and pedagogical competence? Ma's (1999) widely cited study of Chinese math instruction analyzes this issue in depth.

An Incomplete Approach to Fixing the Problem

Much of the debate about the teaching of math, however, seems to focus on only one of these inputs: the design of curricula and the textbooks that encapsulate curricula. Teachers, it is apparently assumed, can quickly present any new curriculum, though the conventional wisdom on teaching practice is that once the classroom door is closed, teachers return to the practices that make sense to them, even if those teaching and learning principles differ from those presented in the mandated textbooks. The debate over textbooks has three components. One concern is how much math overall can be learned by the end of high school and how that total amount of mathematical mastery compares to what is necessary to succeed in college math classes. A second, slightly different, concern is whether the specific math topics taught in high school prepare students for college math courses. Will a mastery of sets and statistics be a good foundation for calculus? Or should more time be spent on algebra and trigonometry? A third concern is how the subject is taught through the textbook. Is math taught at all, in fact, or does the curriculum merely guide students toward discovery of mathematical ideas without ensuring mastery of mathematical procedures?

The sections that follow survey the present world situation in somewhat greater detail with the objectives of introducing some of the key players and of offering further examples of the various schools of thought. The structure of the debate itself helps explain who is interested in dominating science and industry, who is willing to pay for large studies, and which groups most actively spread their views through conferences and through contracting with textbook publishers.

Many nations and their educational leaders do not feel a strong need to participate in the debate; some are satisfied with their educational systems, some are too poor to change, and some are preoccupied with other agendas. Among those who do join the discussion, the Chinese spend the most energy rating world universities and show a strong interest in developing better doctoral education, as demonstrated by the elaborate study of world research productivity carried out each year by Shanghai Jiao Tong University (Shanghai Jiao Tong, World's Top Universities). The Americans spend the most on studies of math education to maintain leadership in technology. The European Community, like China, is working to improve both undergraduate and graduate education through the Bologna process, the discussion of new standards for college degrees that is being carried out by the members of the European Community. South Africa is confronting brain drain, and India the decline of educational productivity outside the most prestigious Indian technical institutes.

These different kinds of national interest in education remind us that the discussion of math education is associated with discussions of many other values. For some, the goal is economic or military dominance; for others, the goal is equity of access to knowledge and jobs; for still others, the goal is to assure that the world remembers its past civilizations and affirms its diversity.

Are Textbooks and Curriculum the Real Issue?

In one common characterization, the traditional math curriculum is a rigorous introduction to the principal topics of mathematics, often presented in historical order, so that (as some parody the curricular design) phylogeny recapitulates ontogeny. In this view, math is a set of building blocks that need each other for support, so it is reasonable to learn math in the order it was invented or discovered. Students learn many algorithms or formulaic techniques for solving problems, and they often learn those techniques without understanding why they work. Dividing fractions by reversing and multiplying is one such algorithm that many students learn without grasping what it really means. One advocate of this approach commented that it is like teaching the proper placement of the hands to a piano student. You don't need to explain that if the student develops sloppy technique he or she will never be able to perform Liszt. You just insist that the student do it the right way. A constructivist may respond, however, that if it only takes a few minutes to show why poor hand position will later limit the performer's ability, why not spend those few minutes to impart a deeper understanding? Why impose rote learning and make a mystery out of something that could easily be explained? Traditionalists will counter that if you gain facility with basic calculations, for example, by memorizing multiplication tables and basic formulae, the student then has the mental "space" necessary to contemplate truly difficult problems.

Traditional Mathematics

American math teaching was taken to task by the public, whether justly or unjustly, after the Soviet Union launched Sputnik in 1957. In retrospect, since America put a person on the moon just eleven years later, the Russian success with Sputnik may not have required changes in American education at all, much less changes such as the experimental math and science curricula that were hastily written and prescribed to American schools. Nor is it clear why new curricula were considered to be the answer, rather than better teacher training or some other modification in education, if education was indeed at fault. At any rate, writing new curricula was the step taken, and the development of math curricula coincided with another development so strange as to be comic. Mathematical theorists at the time found it useful to reconceptualize math in terms of set theory, and a group of French mathematicians, writing under the pseudonym of Monsieur Bourbaki, developed curricula and textbooks for basic math that were grounded in set theory. And that became the New Math. A theoretical insight into the structure of mathematics was turned into a method for teaching every Pierre and Yvette around the world. Were teachers adequately prepared to use this method? Was there good reason to think it superior to traditional methods of teaching?

Reform-based Math

Following New Math came a movement that at least closely tracks the general trends in social values in America and elsewhere. The NCTM curriculum now in print places equity first among values. The teaching mandate is to reach all students, not just the elite. Constructivism, or reform-based math (sometimes called rain forest math and other epithets by its opponents) grew out of the desire to lay a firm foundation for mathematical understanding by helping students of all abilities to understand why mathematical operations work. If writing essays about problems helps, then students should be allowed to write essays. If work with physical models or "manipulatives" helps students to visualize complex ideas, then those will be employed as long as they are useful. If work in groups is helpful, as Uri Triesman's (1992) research showed at Berkeley, then math classes will include opportunities for group problem solving. The Norwegian experience cited on page 12 provides an example of the adoption of constructivism without adequate teacher training. Handing manipulatives to students can result in geometrical insights—or it can result in a classroom of students building houses with sticks if the teacher has not been educated in the method. Worse still, some school districts that have adopted constructivist ideas have actually prohibited students from learning standard skills, such as multiplication tables. Such extremes were never part of any informed educational agenda.

Some scholars consider Dutch Realistic Mathematics Education, known as RME and taking its origin from the Freudenthal Institute at the University of Utrecht, to be a form of constructivism. RME scholars take exception to this characterization, because while RME encourages "guided reinvention" of mathematical ideas, it also requires mastery of traditional skills and algorithms.

Ethnomathematics

The ethnomathematics agenda places a very high value on diversity and therefore emphasizes learning the mathematical traditions of all nations, including the early calendars and mathematical ideas of civilizations long gone. Ethnomathematics is the creation of Ubiritan D'Ambrosio, a Brazilian mathematician. Math has always been a multicultural enterprise. Our "Arabic" numbers come from India, as does the concept of zero. Egypt and Greece gave us geometry; Arabia contributed algebra and many elements of number theory. Italians, the British, the Swiss, Russians, and people from all over Europe, the Americas, and Asia contributed theories and applications. Some nations have made contributions to math that are not present in the standard curricula, and those people may feel they are being victimized or colonized by a foreign subject when they learn math. Therefore, the ethnomathematicians argue, all students should have a chance to understand how their own ancestors developed methods of mathematics. Once students learn that their own ethnic group also created math, they can learn without feeling that the subject is an imposition from outside. Central American children should study the Mayan calendar; African American children should study Harlem street games that involve probability; West Africans should appreciate the complex math implicit in textiles and basket weaving. Underlying this agenda is the assertion that the standard curriculum is not the birthright of all people but rather a form of colonialism.

Ethnomathematical writings raise important political and philosophical questions. To return to the pig and chicken problem, consider that the most important answer may be to ask why the world is so constituted that one farmer can own so many animals while others have none, or to consider how the close relationship between pigs, chickens, and people has led to the transfer of many dangerous diseases to the human population. Many would say such reactions are not math at all; others would respond that focusing on the numerical answer to the problem keeps students from seeing the far more important social issues. Ethnomathematics is not so much an approach to teaching mathematics as a corrective or enrichment of the mathematics curriculum that helps students see connections between math, ethics, politics, geography, history, and other disciplines.

Mathematicians and Mathematics Educators

Another curriculum advocacy group consists of mathematicians and their organizations, but in an odd sense. If one looks at the websites of various national mathematical societies, what strikes one immediately is that very few national math organizations include divisions that focus on K–12 pedagogy. National mathematical societies indeed organize competitions for gifted K–12 students and in some cases address issues in collegiate education. Otherwise, with few exceptions, these societies focus their efforts on theoretical questions. Professional mathematicians and physicists know what they want students to have mastered by the time they reach college; they often express dissatisfaction with the students they encounter; but to a large degree the profession of mathematics appears to be divorced from the profession of teaching math, especially at the primary and secondary levels.

Put simply, mathematicians and math educators don't talk to one another (Ocken 2007). This divorce is not necessarily benign neglect. Sometimes there is absolute hostility expressed by one group for the other, with mathematicians emphasizing the skills necessary to function in advanced fields while math educators explain what is possible when your teaching agenda includes reaching all students, overcoming math anxiety, addressing inequities, and planning curricula for people who will never go to college. Once again, the core issue is elitism versus equity, and the pedagogical issue is what kind of teaching and curricula best serve these different audiences.

The disconnect between professional mathematicians and the teachers of mathematics serves as a microcosm of a larger problem that this book has raised and will raise repeatedly. Is there evidence that any of these curricular models is superior? Can curricula and textbooks be evaluated apart from the work of preparing teachers to understand them and use them effectively? Does the history of the "math wars" or the math debate indicate that math teachers, and their special abilities for fostering abstract mathematical thinking and procedural skills in their students, have been adequately taken into consideration? Or is it the case, rather, that in all the talk and theorizing, all the debate and the sales of textbooks, both the teachers and the students have been left behind?

The Big Tests

The latest round of concern about world math education began with the First International Mathematics Study (FIMS), which was administered in 1964. One can cite earlier dates, such as the Pilot Twelve Country Study of 1959–62, or the later formation of the International Association for the Evaluation of Educational Achievement (IAEEA) in 1967. FIMS was followed by the Second International Mathematics Study (SIMS) in 1980–81. And this, in turn, was followed by the Third International Mathematics and Science Study (TIMSS) in 1995. TIMSS has now morphed into a continuing project called Trends in Math and Science Studies, which may carry out additional worldwide samplings of student math performance.

These large-scale studies were supplemented by other projects sponsored by different international agencies. Particularly notable are the tests called PISA (Program for International

Student Achievement), sponsored by the Organization for Economic Cooperation and Development (OECD), which released results in 1997 and 2001. Some tests focused on math, others on science and reading. These studies were largely funded and led by American, Canadian, British, and European organizations and scholars. Nations dropped in and out of the studies; in some cases, nations that participated did not meet thresholds for numbers of schools or other statistical measures, so their participation was incomplete.

While the results of the studies themselves are reasonably nuanced, the media and politicians picked up chiefly the national rankings, which seemed to show that the major Western industrial powers were falling behind various Asian and Eastern European nations in mathematical ability. What "falling behind" means can be debated, as was noted earlier. The United States is not a standard deviation away from Singapore, for example. Relatively small differences in average raw scores can be made to appear catastrophic, and the data are generally presented in newspapers without much explanation of such important matters as the different types of students tested. As explained earlier, when the full range of American students is compared to graduates of elite math and science academies, the result will always show that the elite students have higher scores.

Scholars outside the Anglo-European orbit have pointed to several other limitations of these global tests. English is the primary language of testing and of the conferences that discuss the results. There seems to be an implicit expectation that the entire world should adopt one arguably superior curriculum, and many fear that that means the imposition of an Anglo-European model on the rest of the world. There is also fear that other international agencies, such as the International Monetary Fund (IMF), will require the adoption of such a curriculum as a condition for relief and loans (Atweh, et al., 2001). And will third world nations be used to test potentially ineffective programs? What of the heavy reliance on technology in some of the new teaching designs? How can computerized instruction be paid for and updated in nations where the average citizen earns a few dollars a day or less?

Broadly speaking, the nations that paid for these tests, and whose citizens appeared to demonstrate only modest performance, have set to work on additional studies, legislation, and curricular reforms. Most of the subsequent conferences on these topics have been hosted in these same nations, with limited attendance by representatives from the poorer sections of the globe.

Macnab (2000) from Northern College in Aberdeen, Scotland, has published a careful review of what nations have done with the results of the TIMSS tests. Using questionnaires and other data from the 40 nations that participated in the tests, 19 of which did not meet all the TIMSS criteria for participation, Macnab identified 23 nations that started down the road to some kind of educational change. Fourteen of the 23 countries made a "national response." In most cases, this consisted of the publication of a national report. Fewer nations organized countrywide or regional conferences. Seven formed "policy groups to promote change." Two nations were considering policy initiatives, and only three nations or parts of nations had started "development projects": the United States, Norway, and Flemish Belgium.

Macnab's summary indicates that the UK and New Zealand also initiated curricular reviews and articulated new standards. France and Sweden had changes underway before TIMSS. Macnab's research also points to the problems created by a lack of centralization of educational planning in such federally organized nations as Canada and the United States, whose federal governments have no power to mandate national math standards or policies.

Categorizing these results, Macnab observes that among the nations that participated, "not all countries made use of this opportunity; of those that did, not all were prepared to accept what was revealed; and that among those who did accept the verdict of TIMSS, there was not agreement as to the nature and depth of the changes required" (p. 13).

Howson (1999), a senior consultant to several international studies, has commented that "it is by no means easy to make significant changes in a beneficial way" (p. 167). Howson's observation may seem utterly banal until one considers that much of the international discussion of math education has assumed that changes in textbooks, curricula, teacher training, teacher in-service education, and the mathematical thinking of teachers and students can be accomplished in short periods of time.

Howson concluded that the real value of comparative tests and studies lies in the willingness of good teachers from similar cultures to consult with one another about ways to teach more effectively. This insight has many components. First, it reinforces Ma's conclusion that dialogue among teachers is critical and Ball's conclusion, discussed extensively in a later chapter, that the key to good math teaching is for teachers to share insights about instructing complex numerical and abstract concepts. Second, Howson's conclusion means that comparisons among nations that have dissimilar cultures are not pedagogically useful. The British and Americans will not start parenting like the Japanese or Koreans. However, conversations between teachers in Washington State and Alberta or British Columbia might be very useful on all sides. Further, Howson's analysis speaks to the importance of change that comes from teachers, not from policymakers or outside experts. He supports his conclusions with references to a number of consultations that have taken place among teachers in Europe. Finally, Howson points out that these low-tech meetings, conversations, or consultations among teachers within a school system, or between teachers in neighboring districts or nations, can accomplish a great deal at relatively low cost.

The Canadian Mathematics Education Study Group sponsors precisely this kind of conversation. As the organization emphasizes in its invitations, this is a "conference based on conferring." Working groups share perspectives and teaching points; some working groups are set aside for senior practitioners, others for beginning teachers, and there are also "ad hoc sessions" that can be organized to treat any emerging idea (Canadian Mathematics Education Study Group, 2006).

Perhaps the most severe critique of international mega-tests has been written by Keitel and Kilpatrick (1999) in their essay "Rationality and Irrationality of International Comparisons." After pointing out how reports of average scores, without any reference to standard deviations or the meaning of the differences in scores, lead to useless rank-ordered lists of nations, and after making several observations similar to Howson's about the limited use of comparisons between cultures with radically different approaches to childhood and personal choice, Keitel and Kilpatrick raise a number of additional issues. What correlations, if any, exist among scores on the one hand and important output measures like degrees earned, patents issued, publications in leading journals, or national economic health? Those who are concerned about the international rankings express fear that a low ranking means that creativity or economic standing is draining away, but there are no studies that show such causal connections.

Keitel and Kilpatrick focus their criticism of the big tests on what they call irrational conclusions made by interpreters of the test results. "TIMSS," they write, "threatens to poison for some time the waters of educational policy, as politicians and researchers scramble to take advantage of what TIMSS allegedly says about the teaching and learning of mathematics in their country. . . . International comparative studies are trumpeted in educational journals and the press as triumphs of rationality. . . . Researchers conducting the studies have too much vested in the outcomes to engage in sufficient reflection about the foundations of their work" (Keitel and Kilpatrick 1999). This judgment is worth keeping in mind because of the extent to which those who organize and support studies and particular positions on math education are linked to particular foundations and textbook companies. Their concerns also point to the importance of keeping perspective. If nations are persuaded that they are on the brink of a crisis, or are about to fail in the international economic competition, they may be less able or willing to address issues of educational equity. As will be made clear in the next chapter, this is an issue at the heart of the American discussion of math.

How Do Responses to the Tests Play Out in National Curricula?

This section offers a bird's-eye view of recommendations for improving math education from the world's various curricular camps. Our intent is to give a sense of the breadth of opinion and the passion with which these views are held.

Ethnomathematics Revisited

An extreme challenge to traditionalism and constructivism comes from ethnomathematics. Two advocates of this view are worth quoting at length to give a flavor of this side of the debate. "It goes without saying that the mathematics of the 21st century has allowed impressive scientific achievements to emerge in all parts of the planet, yet this came with incalculable costs to the millions of people, their cultures and civilizations as European/North American ideas, morality and science have come to dominate and control, and capture our imagination. It has, as well, enabled some of the most horrific, social, scientific, ecological and cultural disasters in the history of the planet. The Ethnomathematics Program considers a concept of mathematics which includes a critical, moral, holistic, and global perspective. That is, a mathematics curriculum that 'walks the mystical way with practical feet'" (Orey and Rosa 2006).

Davidson (1990), writing about teaching Native Americans, suggests that students with high math scores may in fact know very little about math, which is evident when one asks them to write essays on the subject. Conversely, students who can write essays about mathematical questions may have an equally important, though different, mathematical knowledge. From the perspective of these authors, it might follow that math teachers should obtain more training in political theory, contemporary liberation ideologies, and comparative ethical and cultural systems. More pointedly, Frankenstein from the University of Massachusetts sees ethnomathematics as a means for combating capitalism: "We believe that major objectives of all education are to shatter myths about how society is structured; to understand the effects of, and interconnections among racism, sexism, ageism, heterosexism, monopoly capitalism, imperialism and other alienating, totalitarian institutional structures and attitudes; to develop the commitment to rebuild those structures and attitudes; and, to develop the personal and collective empowerment to engage that task" (Frankenstein n.d.).

Ubiratan D'Ambrosio, founder of ethnomathematics, once defined the issue in these words written for the *Chronicle of Higher Education*: "Mathematics is absolutely integrated with Western civilization, which conquered and dominated the entire world. The only possibility of building up a planetary civilization depends on restoring the dignity of the losers and, together, winners and losers, moving into the new. [Ethno-mathematics] is a step toward peace" (Greene 2000). Here D'Ambrosio offers a vision of his field that differs from another formulation he has offered, which recognizes that mathematics is in fact the creation of all societies, with contributions from many nations and peoples well outside what is generally considered Western civilization.

Ethnomathematicians (as well as others) also express concern about the digital divide. Computers are not necessary for basic education, and to the extent that some European and American textbooks and educational systems encourage the use of advanced technology, those systems of education can prove too expensive for poor nations (Koblitz 1996)). On the world scene, ethnomathematics is particularly important both in Brazil and in Portugal, which have large immigrant populations and a deep concern for improving the educational opportunity of minority populations. Ethnomathematics does not offer a curricular model for teaching math or for training teachers how to teach math. It does not offer an alternative mathematics. In fact, the extremity of its challenge to both traditional and reform-based math instruction lies in the claim that learning to quantify, measure, and manipulate the world has led to warfare, colonialism, and genocide, so that it might have been preferable if there were no math at all. Ethnomathematics, however, does offer a supplemental curriculum focused on human values.

Constructivism Revisited

Constructivism, sometimes called the new-new math, has in fact been around for a long time in other forms. The Park City Math Conference in Utah and its predecessor conferences, associated with the Princeton Institute for Advanced Studies, have been working with talented American teachers for decades to develop math education programs that produce graduates who have excellent abilities not merely in all the traditional math skills, but also in individual and group problem-solving. Top American prep schools, such as the Philips Exeter Academy in New Hampshire, have used a small-group, constructivist approach to teaching math and other subjects since their founding (Mallinson 2007).

Constructivism is now the dominant theoretical model in Anglo-American math education, as it is in other areas of education as well, though one view is that the battle between traditionalists and constructivists is to an important degree a battle over a straw man, because no one knows enough about what actually goes on in classrooms or what kinds of pedagogical knowledge the best teachers have. To put this another way, just because one theory of education has perhaps displaced another theory, and just because textbooks may now be written more out of one theoretical perspective than another, there is no reason to conclude that teaching and learning in the classroom reflect any particular model. In the United States, the websites of such groups as "Mathematicallycorrect" (on the traditionalist side) and "Mathematicallysane" (on the constructivist side) trade salvos as if it were abundantly clear what teachers have been well trained to do, and as if we knew how math was, in fact, being taught. An international perspective is helpful precisely because it allows us to see how the same battles are played out in the same hot language across the world. A recent Presidential Commission of Enquiry into Education in Zimbabwe concluded that the British model of education had failed, pointed to the "international disaster" of New Math, and argued simultaneously for creative teaching, avoidance of memorization, and the importance of teaching strict mathematical proofs (Memorandum to Presidential Commission of Enquiry into Education, n.d.). The Commission's list of targets includes most of the slogans of both traditionalism and constructivism. Keele University's "Thinking Maths" program in the UK offers one definition of the constructivist approach. "While each lesson has a clear agenda involving fundamental concepts in mathematics, the lesson does not focus directly on pupils learning these concepts, but rather on them 'struggling on the way' towards these concepts. The emphasis is on pupils in small groups, individually, or in whole-class discussion, producing formulations and gaining insights at different levels of complexity, all related to the concepts. The outcome of the lesson is the thinking process and the sharing of ideas rather than the specific knowledge and the skills themselves" (Keele University n.d., p. 1.). A traditionalist might well point out that it would be good if the outcome of each lesson was both the thinking process and specific knowledge and skills. Many constructivists would agree that the point is both/and, not either/or.

One American version of reform-based curriculum is the "Connected Mathematics Project" that was developed at Michigan State University from 1991 to 1997 on the basis of the standards recommended by the National Council of Teachers of Mathematics (NCTM). The website for this curriculum explains that the approach is problem centered, involves the teacher as a guide, and requires that the teacher have a deep knowledge of mathematics. Connected Math provides teacher training materials. At issue, of course, is whether we know enough yet about that pedagogical knowledge, which is part of the current research agenda at MSU. How many teachers have a sufficiently deep knowledge? This is not solely an American issue. A recent report from the Czech Republic makes the same point. Stehlikova and Hejny of Charles University describe how difficult it is for experienced math teachers to change their methods, which is the same point made by Stigler and Hiebert of UCLA about the very complex task of changing a dynamic educational system that is already in place and fully staffed with teachers of varying abilities

(Stehlikova and Hejny 1999, Stigler and Hiebert 1997).

If, as mentioned earlier, Norway is the poster child for the problems of introducing a constructivist curriculum without adequate teacher training (Braams 2002), the poster child for the success of constructivism may be the Netherlands, whose scores on the various international tests have remained high. The complete Dutch model of math education, based on the Freudenthal Institute's Realistic Mathematics Education program (RME), joins both a constructivist inquiry model of learning with rich opportunities to learn and practice traditional algorithms, problem-solving techniques, multiplication tables, and other skills (Hanlon 1998, van den Heuvel-Panhuizen 2000). Many scholars have emphasized this distinction between constructivism and RME, including Zulkardi et al. (n.d.) and Widjaja (2004) in Indonesia. Other scholars have assessed the difficulty of moving from a rigidly structured traditionalism that emphasizes rote learning to any model that requires teachers to lead inquiry and to have enough knowledge of math, and enough special pedagogical ability in the teaching of mathematical ideas, to make the transition from traditionalism to either RME or constructivism. Monteiro and Pinto (n.d.) in Brazil, Fletcher (2005) of the University of Cape Coast in Ghana, and Zanzali (2003) in Malaysia all make similar observations that training teachers to use new methods is difficult and that often, as Zanzali writes, "the constructive nature of learning mathematics inherent in the curriculum is not reflected in classroom teaching" (p. 37).

Ellis and Berry (2005) take a different perspective on constructivism by asserting that it is a work in progress rather than a complete curriculum. They term the traditionalist approach the "procedural-formalist paradigm" and the newer approach the "cognitive-cultural paradigm." As the new paradigm develops, they judge that curriculum designers and teachers "deliberately refrain from issuing rigid prescriptions for classroom practices and static lists of criteria for measuring learning, opting instead to share varied descriptions of learning environments and multiple examples of the sorts of outcomes to be expected." An example of this broad approach to creating constructivist education can be found in the agenda of the Mathematics Education into the 21st Century Project (n.d.), which began in 1986. The conferences held by this group are designed to produce a "Super Course" in math that includes "problem solving, use of technology, new ways of assessment, ways of dealing with cultural differences, overcoming gender and social barriers, improving the curriculum, teacher preparation and ongoing development, policy initiatives, school organization, classroom practices, using statistics in everyday life, effectively utilizing new paradigms in teaching and learning, rich learning tasks, applications of mathematics and modeling in the real world, and computer graphics." One cannot contemplate such a large agenda without reflecting on which issues are most basic and on what most nations can afford. The Government of Bhutan publication (Dorji 2006) offers the perspective of a poor nation; the guide for teachers written by Grouws and Cebulla (2001) and published by the International Academy of Education, with support from UNESCO, provides another example of how teachers might be prepared to offer a broader form of math education that can address the needs of citizens in both technology-rich and technology-poor nations.

Is constructivism a description of the way that truly excellent math education has been offered for centuries? Is it a work in progress? Does it truly lack attention to the basics offered by RME and traditionalism? Does it assume too much content and pedagogical knowledge from math teachers who in many cases across the world have limited math education? If there is a problem, is it a problem of theory, of curriculum, or of attention to what teachers need to know to convey this complex subject? A brief survey of the literature on tradition-alism offers both a critique of the other major trends in the world and an opportunity to examine whether traditionalism has answered its critics.

Traditionalism Revisited

Traditionalism is an appropriate place to end this chapter, because the advocates of traditional mathematics teaching, however that may be defined, play a large role in the American debate over math, which is the subject of the next chapter. It is not clear whether advocates of traditional approaches have proposals for solving all of the perceived problems that the other curricular theories are trying to address, such as making math more accessible to women and minorities or helping average students to understand the underlying logic of stan-dard algorithms. Nor does traditionalism necessarily have an answer to the teaching problems created by the sheer expan-sion of knowledge. As was noted earlier, students today may wish to learn quaternions, Taylor series, and fractal geometry to do graphics programming. The NCTM recommends more statistics, which gets more attention in Europe and which is useful to citizens and researchers alike. If these topics are added, then what must be cut, and where (Warfield September 18, 2007)?

Traditionalists often frame their contribution to the math debate in four ways. First, they make comparisons between the high scores of Asian nations and the lower scores of Anglo-American countries. Some traditionalists, particularly those who home-school, tend to adopt textbooks from Singapore to try to capture the excellent results of Asian teaching, some-times without considering the differences both in parenting and in the training of math teachers and also without noting that Singapore itself is moving toward the adoption of a more constructivist approach. Second, traditionalists argue that the constructivist curriculum does not give enough attention to learning basic skills and methods, so that students leave high school with far less knowledge than past generations. Third, traditionalists call for the mastery of a standard curriculum whose outlines are sometimes merely implied. At an absolute minimum, this curriculum includes memorizing multiplication tables, pencil and paper methods for basic operations, basic geometry, proofs, and standard formulae for common mathematical problems, so that all students can take algebra in 8th grade and have the potential to learn calculus either in high school or college. Calculus is considered the goal by American traditionalists, whereas constructivists in the U.S., like most European teachers of math, set a goal of spending more classroom time on statistics and applied math. Fourth, traditionalists express concern about the falling numbers of U.S. students taking degrees in math and science.

Critics of this traditionalist agenda observe that while these methods apparently work well for elite students, they do not necessarily serve less talented students very well. The core philosophical issue is, therefore, equity. As we have hypothesized before, the other issues are that elite students may have been exposed to a constructivist approach to teaching all along, and it is not clear what theory of teaching is actually being lived out in the world's classrooms because teacher training and in-service work have not kept pace with theory and textbook development.

Studies of what happens in international classrooms have produced a variety of results. McNaught and Won's 2006 study of Korean and American education found that five factors explained 56% of the variation between the teaching styles of the classrooms studied, yet their research did not look at teachers' backgrounds. Ma's now famous study (1999) of the differences between Chinese and American math teachers, by contrast, focused precisely on teacher training and teacher assignments. She found that Chinese teachers had extensive backgrounds in math, could answer math problems that most American teachers could not solve, and spent their careers teaching only math. These research findings are reinforced by a study performed on an American school district that adopted Singaporean math texts in the hope of reproducing Singapore's high math scores. While three of the schools in the district showed higher scores, many of the schools in the experiment dropped out. Garelick (2006), an advocate for traditionalism who evaluated the experiment, found that problems with the texts included a poor fit to the state tests, a lack of contextualized examples, and a lack of teacher preparation. Singaporean teachers, he concluded, also had more knowledge of math—a point that tallies with Ma's findings.

Ahuja (2006) of Kent State University offered a useful set of recommendations based on his study of traditionalism and the other theories currently on offer in the world. He calls for a combination of the traditionalist and constructivist paradigms, development of textbooks that convey this joint paradigm, attention to issues of educational equity, and efforts to assure that the world's math classrooms are filled with well-trained, highly honored, and well-compensated teachers.

A Different Conclusion

One observation in the face of this information about the world debate is that, after the various paradigms and theories are compared, the discussion always gravitates back to what teachers know about math and what excellent teachers know about how to teach math. There is a difference between knowing math very well and having a vocabulary, a set of examples, the ability to assess student difficulties, and other skills that make one a superb instructor of mathematical ideas. The other key issues in the world debate concern the content of the curriculum—whether calculus, practical math, statistics, or applied math, and for which students—and the issue of educational equity—how all students will be taught well, not just an elite. Finally, as Stigler and Hiebert and others have stated often, changes to math teaching never take place in a vacuum. Any innovations must take into consideration the existing systems of teacher selection, teacher preparation, in-service learning, student preparation, parental understanding of the curriculum, and many other social and cultural factors. But, above all, it is clear that the math teacher is the most important link. We know too little about what math teachers know, and we need to learn much more about the best practices of the most gifted math teachers on the planet.

2

The American Dilemma

Now that we have a sense of the larger issues in the world of mathematics education, we turn to a discussion of the influences that contribute to or distract from our national capacity to improve mathematics education and, as a result, improve student learning of mathematics. You can hardly pick up a newspaper or news magazine, let alone professional journals or articles offered by scholarly commentators, without finding rallying cries for schools to improve student achievement in dynamic ways. Many policy makers, educators, and members of the public see our country's current status—often referred to as a crisis with respect to international comparisons of student performance in mathematics—as unacceptable and a precursor of certain economic doom. This perception has characterized the collective view of mathematics education in this country for many years.

In 1981, Secretary of Education T. H. Bell created the National Commission on Excellence in Education in response to "the widespread public perception that something is seriously remiss in our educational system" (National Commission on Excellence in Education 1983). The commission's report, titled *A Nation at Risk*, summarized the evidence for concern and proposed improvements. Reforms since 1983 have been led by government agencies and have focused on raising standards and improving teaching to enhance student performance (Martin and Crowell 2000). President George W.

Bush's Elementary and Secondary Education Act of 2001, also known as the No Child Left Behind Act (NCLB), was passed in 2002 and has four principles: "accountability for results; local control and flexibility; enhanced parental choice; and effective and successful programs." These principles do not self-evidently mandate what constitutes success or effectiveness, so it is fair to ask, successful for whom and as measured by what standards?

Since the 1880s, one of the goals of American education has been to prepare people for different career paths. The NCLB was designed to secure high levels of achievement for all students. From the standpoint of many educational researchers, the mandate to serve all students opened an opportunity to apply the latest theories about human learning, such as described in various government reports and educational research literature, including *How People Learn: Brain, Mind, Experience, and School* (National Research Council 1999a) and *How People Learn: Bridging Research and Practice* (National Research Council 1999b), and supported by cognitive research, such as Caine and Caine's *Making Connections: Teaching the Human Brian* (1991). These documents describe principles of "powerful teaching and learning" that have been adopted throughout the nation and also in Washington State, and the principles are sometimes called reform-based education or constructivism. On this model the teacher attends to the individual learning needs of each student and creates a learner-centered environment where students learn through hands-on involvement and real-life situations (Sutherland 1992). Hyerle (1996) called this shift in thinking about the classroom a "cognitive revolution" (p. 13) that takes education away from rote behaviorism. Newmann and Wehlage (1993) divided this "authentic" approach to education into five components: 1) higher-order thinking, 2) depth of knowledge, 3) connectedness to the world, 4) substantive conversation, and 5) social support for student achievement. All of these require alternative assessments. Although the theoretical model of education and the assessment strategies changed, instructional practices did not necessarily change (Baker, Gratama, and Bachtler 2002; Baker, Gratama, and Bachtler 2003). Nor did many citizens' expectations for the content of math education or their opinions about how math ought to be taught, according to a research study (Davis, 2007) quoted in *Education Week*, entitled "Parents Less Worried Than Experts Over Math, Science."

What Is the Problem?

In the United States, many people say that they "just aren't good at math." Moreover, they feel no embarrassment about this self-analysis. While these same people may not be good readers, they are unlikely to admit it, because illiteracy is equated with ignorance, lack of education, and even stupidity.

Why is it acceptable to do poorly at math but not at reading? Based on our review of the national literature on mathematics and math education, we offer four explanations. First, people think *mathematics is something you are good at because you were born that way.* In a public opinion survey conducted in Washington and Massachusetts (Mass Insight Education and Research Institute, April 2004), over a third of the adults surveyed agreed that "even many smart people don't have the ability to learn math." Unfortunately, many teachers also believe that a large proportion of the student population cannot learn math, even with good instruction. Second, many adults believe that *all you need is "shopkeeper arithmetic."* Experts can do higher level math for you, so there is no need for students to be proficient in algebra, geometry, statistics, and other topics mandated in state and federal standards. Third, *math is a subject where only the elite will ever shine.* Educators should therefore sort out those people, wash out the rest, and even stop providing remediation at the college level for those who don't get it. Fourth, *math should be studied at an advanced level only by those who are going into math-intensive careers* such as computer science, physics, economics, engineering, and rocket science. The only good reason to raise the bar for all students is to assure that in the end the nation has enough of these talented people to fill the jobs in math-intensive fields.

A less commonly held view about math is that it is the "language of the physical world." Some adults discover math later in life and find that it is enjoyable and eminently useful. Teachers who align themselves with the NCTM goals include those who had poor learning experiences when they were children but later developed a love for math through teacher education programs and professional development activities. These teachers have a passionate commitment to reforming math education to make it accessible to all learners from an early age, before children can develop negative attitudes.

Given these opinions of mathematics as a subject, it is no wonder that the United States, like other nations, has such difficulty deciding what math ought to be studied and what level of proficiency ought to be obtained by which students. As pointed out in the first chapter, a key issue in this discussion is whether educational equity should be the goal or whether the objective is to train an elite. In either case, it seems that teachers' attitudes, as well as their competence, lie at the heart of instruction.

Instructional Issues

Educators agree that improving math achievement presents more complex challenges than improving literacy (Mass Insight Education and Research Institute, May 2004). Producing highly capable math students requires instruction that enables them to think abstractly about quantitative information and to work easily with complex calculations that include many steps. A majority of teachers, however, appear to believe that math is procedural and formulaic, with questions that have one answer and only one way of getting to that answer (Ma 1999, Stigler and Hiebert 1999). Even many mathematicians believe that this traditional, formulaic approach to learning math is the best. Teachers still tell students that all of math boils down to adding, subtracting, multiplying, and dividing. This view does not align with the emerging technical economy, nor does it further the goal of preparing all students to think skillfully about the quantitative aspects of the world and their work. The ongoing attempts by the NCTM, the NRC, and other organizations to broaden the content and methods of math instruction therefore face a continuing backlash to return to the basics, whatever those basics are understood to be (National Council of Teachers of Mathematics 2000, National Research Council 2001).

American math education is also impacted by what some research literature refers to as the "happiness factor." U.S. educators have made self-confidence, relevance, and joy of learning important goals in instruction. Most American parents want their children to like school and be confident and capable. But as the Third International Mathematics and Science Study (TIMSS) data have shown, happiness is not a high priority in some nations that demonstrate high math achievement. In fact, the more math a child knows, the less likely he or she is to be happy about learning math (Loveless 2006). Constructivist approaches to learning, which leave students groping for answers, can produce far less satisfaction than curricula that provide formulaic answers.

Continuous demands for change and for compliance with one new set of standards after another, whether those of the NCLB or, in Washington State, the Washington Assessment of Student Learning (WASL), have further impacted American math education. Werner Heisenberg's basic principle of observation applies here: doing an experiment changes the reality. In the United States, new curricula have seldom been given much time to succeed, and teachers have not been prepared to carry out their ever-changing assignments. We have no patience for incremental improvement in schools, we give little time for reforms to produce results, we want immediate gratification, and we tend to blame someone if positive change does not result quickly. Consequently, the pendulum of reform swings from one fad to another, parents complain about their children becoming lab rats, and educators retreat into the conviction that "this too shall pass." Michael Fullan, a researcher and leader in the study of educational change, has been telling us for two decades that institutionalization of any big change takes at least three to five years, with an "implementation dip" that occurs once reform efforts are seriously launched. Often, due to the backlash that inevitably occurs, school leaders will abandon new instructional programs or move to different strategies that critics may find more acceptable, before fully trying out what was attempted in the first place (Fullan 1993, 2001, 2003, 2008). This is perhaps one explanation related to our critical insights about first-order and second-order change. In a later chapter, we address what it takes to sustain large-scale reform.

Haves and Have Nots: The Issue of Equity

Mathematics education has become a civil rights issue because proficiency in mathematics is critical for entering many professions with higher pay and status. "Math has long been recognized as a critical filter. Coursework in math has traditionally been a gateway to technological literacy and to higher education" (Schoenfeld 2002, p. 13). Disproportionate numbers of poor and minority students perform below math standards. For this and other reasons, the NCLB targeted four subgroups for particular attention in "closing the achievement gap": the poor, ESL students, racial and ethnic minorities, and students who require special education. What can schools do differently to address these needs? The National Council of Teachers of Mathematics (NCTM) placed equity first in its list of objectives in the *Principles and Standards for School Mathematics* (2000). How to achieve that goal continues to be a controversial educational and cultural issue. Efforts to equalize access to high-quality math education are hampered in many ways. For example, research from one district in Texas indicates that low achieving students are far more likely to be assigned to ineffective teachers than to effective teachers (Hall and Kennedy 2006). We will return to this issue, and to evidence of a different kind, in the next chapter.

A deeper analysis of this issue is offered by Stigler and Hiebert's *The Teaching Gap* (1999), which assesses and reflects upon the results of the TIMSS. They conclude that "cultural activities are represented in cultural scripts, generalized knowledge about an event that resides in the heads of participants. These scripts guide behavior and also tell participants what to expect. Within a culture, these scripts are widely shared, and therefore they are hard to see" (p. 85). Teaching is one such cultural activity, they claim, and they illustrate their point by contrasting teaching and learning methods in the United States and Japan, with an emphasis on the different cultural beliefs about education. According to Stigler and Hiebert (1999), American teachers believe that school mathematics is a set of procedures for solving problems and that learning terms and practicing skills is not exciting but is just something that students must do. Japanese teachers approach math differently. They think of mathematics as a set of relationships among concepts, facts, and procedures, and they feel their students should find it inherently interesting to explore those relationships and to develop new skills for thinking about those concepts. American teachers believe math is "learned best by mastering the material incrementally" and that "confusion and frustration . . . should be minimized" (p. 90). Japanese teachers believe, instead, that learning must involve frustration and confusion. American teachers "act as if confusion and frustration are signs that they have not done their job" (p. 92).

Japanese and American teachers also have divergent perspectives on individual differences among students. In the U.S., individual differences are viewed as obstacles, because meeting every student's needs involves diagnosing student ability and providing different levels of instruction, which is difficult in large classes. The Japanese view individual differences as a natural part of any group of learners and as a resource in problem-solving (p. 94). Stigler and Hiebert note that American and Japanese teachers tend to use visual aids differently, too. American teachers use an overhead projector as a means for keeping all students focused on the teacher's presentation, whereas Japanese teachers tend to use the chalkboard to develop answers with the participation of the class. These generalizations are not absolute, of course, and part of what we discuss in the next chapter is the evidence that there are some excellent American teachers, including teachers in Washington State, who in fact are skilled in working with student differences and in helping groups of students learn together in spite of significant differences in their mathematical ability and their approach to problems.

Stigler and Hiebert summarize their findings by saying that "if teaching were a non-cultural activity, we could try to improve it simply by providing better information in teachers' manuals, or asking experts to demonstrate better techniques, or distributing written recommendations on more effective teaching methods. Note that this is exactly what we have been doing" (p. 101). They conclude that we have not focused on teaching itself because of its constant, deeply rooted cultural nature. "Teaching is so constant within our own culture that we fail even to imagine how it might be changed, much less believe that it should be changed" (p. 103). Current research suggests that the gap between the mathematically gifted and the rest of us cannot be bridged until the way Americans teach and think of teaching math is changed at a deep cultural level.

Can All Students Master Math?

Some scholars believe all students can learn mathematics. "The research over the past two decades . . . convinces us that all students can learn to think mathematically. There are instances of schools scattered throughout the country in which a high percentage of students have high levels of achievement in mathematics. Further, there have also been special interventions in disadvantaged schools whereby students have made substantial progress" (National Research Council 2001, p. 16). A recent report (Kitchen et al. 2007) entitled *Mathematics Education at Highly Effective Schools that Serve the Poor*, concluded that there exist three major aspects of schools that "overcame injustices associated with poverty" (p. 3). These are: high expectations (although what "high expectations" actually means is unclear), challenging mathematical content and high-level instruction, and the importance of building relationships among teachers. These findings are consistent with the research conducted by the Washington School Research Center, which is the focus of the next chapter. Kitchen et al. write further that, in unsuccessful schools, "instead of stressing high-level thinking and the development of students' critical thinking skills, the focus has been on instruction of rote skills for success on standardized tests. This has led to low educational expectations, which has catastrophic consequences for [students in poverty]" (p. 2).

Math education may boil down to this: if you teach them, they will learn. But first, teachers need to agree on what they will teach, and second, teachers need to determine whether they know how to teach that content. Some criticism is directed toward teachers and teacher education to the effect that teachers do not know enough content and are not getting it from their teacher education programs (see, e.g., Greenberg and Walsh 2008). Yet the American debate over educational standards focuses on only one of these components: what is to be taught.

Mathematics Standards in the United States

The United States differs from most other nations in that our math standards are determined state by state rather than by the nation as a whole. To address the diversity of state standards, and to establish comprehensive learning goals for math, the National Council of Teachers of Mathematics published its *Curriculum and Evaluation Standards for School Mathematics* in 1989. NCTM was the first professional organization to define learning goals in terms of a set of standards, and this document was followed by additional publications: *Professional Standards for Teaching Mathematics* (NCTM 1991) and *Assessment Standards for School Mathematics* (NCTM 1995). Each of these documents has been revised over the past decade of implementation and evaluation.

NCTM's 2000 publication, *Principles and Standards for School Mathematics*, pulled together everything that had been learned since 1989. The updated version is supplemented by a *Research Companion* (NCTM 2003) that provides support and justification for NCTM's positions, something that was lacking in the first edition. In 2005, NCTM published *Standards and Curriculum: A View from the Nation*. This document was developed with the assistance of the Park City Math Conference and the Association of State Supervisors of Mathematics. In the preface, the book states that "The movement to develop state standards has continued, and it appears that the United States has come closer than ever before to having a de facto national curriculum" (p. 1). NCTM's still more recent *Curriculum Focal Points for Prekindergarten through Grade 8 Mathematics: A Quest for Coherence* (2006), responds to further calls for clarity in the approach to standards, although early childhood mathematics educators worry that children's cognitive development can be negatively affected in the attempt to implement tightly specified grade level expectations for prekindergarten and primary grades (Richardson 2008).

The underlying principles of the 2000 *Principles and Standards for School Mathematics* are: equity, a well-articulated curriculum, teaching with understanding of what students know, learning with a deep understanding, assessment that supports learning, and technology that enhances student learning (p. 6). The NCTM standards are "descriptions of what mathematics instruction should enable students to know and do" (p. 7). There are content standards and process standards. The five content standards specify learning goals in the areas of:

- Number and operations, including the basic operations, number systems, and estimating
- Algebra, including symbolic representation of unknowns
- Geometry, including two- and three-dimensional shapes and methods of representing spatial relationships
- Measurement
- Data analysis and probability, including basic statistics and statistical inferences.

Under each of these headings the standards offer specific expectations for each group of grade levels: Pre K–2, 3–5, 6–8, and 9–12.

The five process standards define the mathematical reasoning and problem solving skills that should be developed by all students. These include:

- Problem-solving
- Reasoning and proofs
- Communication of mathematical ideas to others
- Connections, meaning the ability to see connections among mathematical ideas and to apply those ideas both within math and to problems that are in contexts outside of formal mathematics
- Representation, or the ability to use multiple methods of representing mathematical ideas and their application to other contexts

Although the NCTM did not set out to establish a single national standard, much of the activity in U.S. mathematics education since 1989 has been defined by responses to the NCTM documents, which are characterized by such curricular recommendations as downplaying the role of rote learning and emphasizing a variety of approaches to problem solving. Many states have based their standards on the NCTM standards, often with little adaptation. At the same time, the individual states have created high stakes achievement tests to assess students' ability to meet the standards. The important point here is that the emphasis has been on setting standards and evaluating students. Textbook companies have produced materials based on the standards and have published teacher's manuals, but little attention has been paid to what teachers know, how they might actually teach these materials, and what systems of support teachers need to teach this or any other form of mathematics with greater proficiency.

Traditionalism or Constructivism?

It is appropriate to comment here that from the perspective of the two most important groups of educational theorists, the traditionalists and the constructivists, the NCTM standards raise many hotly debated issues. Should problem-solving be taught by traditional rote learning, or should it also include opportunities for experimentation with other approaches if those approaches help students learn the material deeply? How much time should be spent on formal proofs when even mathematical experts disagree about the meaning of proofs? How important are group work and writing exercises that help students learn how to communicate their approaches to problems? And if such communication is not a top priority, how will the next generation of math teachers learn to convey their insights to the next generation of students?

Adoption and implementation of the NCTM standards varies from state to state, and many states have revised their standards repeatedly over the last decade or more. Observing these changes, the National Research Council's 2001 report, *Adding It Up*, commented that "the fragmentation of these standards, their multiple sources, and the limited conceptual frameworks on which they rest have not resulted in a coherent, well-articulated, widely accepted set of learning goals for U.S. school mathematics" (p. 36). In 2005, the Fordham Foundation, which strongly advocates a traditionalist approach, evaluated the various states' standards (Klein 2005). The Fordham scholars gave low grades to states that were aligned with the National Assessment of Educational Progress (NAEP) because, in their view, that assessment was based on the 1989 NCTM standards. California and Massachusetts, which diverged most from the NAEP guidelines, received the highest grades (Loveless 2006). Washington State received an F; this grade has been reported often, particularly by those who advocate traditional approaches to math education. But as we have stated previously, it is not clear what is going on in the classrooms of Washington or any other state, because passing standards, publishing textbooks, offering limited in-service training, and writing state-wide tests leave out both the teachers and the process of teaching itself. Those who blame test results on one approach to teaching or another might be surprised by an inventory of what was actually being taught. But we do not have such an inventory.

Mathematics Assessment

More testing has been required as a result of legislation such as NCLB, but is there reason to believe that more testing results in better instruction? Many educators doubt it. As Auty (1994), an assessment coordinator in Oregon, once put it, "testing students is like sticking a thermometer into a turkey as you're fixing Thanksgiving dinner; you can find out how done it is, but taking its temperature doesn't cook it." Schoenfeld (2002), an educational researcher at the University of California, Berkeley, puts it this way: "Stakeholders in the educational system have to understand the great variability inherent in testing. People put great faith in the stability of test scores . . . most people attribute significant meanings to particular test scores and to minor variations in them. In fact, test-retest differences on almost all standardized tests can be substantial . . . the public needs to understand . . . that gains in test scores are often illusory or artifactual, and that high-stakes testing can result both in curricular deformation and in the loss of intrinsic motivation for students" (p. 23).

In the United States, the confusion surrounding test scores has been increased by the (perceived) "dumbing down" of SAT scores in 2005 and by various states' decisions to change what constitutes a passing score on high-stakes tests introduced either before or since the passage of NCLB (Cech 2007). A brief review of the major tests illustrates these difficulties of interpretation.

The Third International Mathematics and Science Study (TIMSS) of 1995 was described in the previous chapter. One of the key problems with TIMSS data is that a representative sample of American students has been compared in many cases to samples drawn from elite academies in other nations. Within the United States, a key assessment is the NAEP, the National Assessment of Educational Progress, which calls itself "The Nation's Report Card." According to its website (http://nces.ed.gov/nationsreportcard/), "The National Assessment of Educational Progress is the only nationally representative and continuing assessment of what America's students know and can do in various subject areas. Assessments are conducted periodically in mathematics, reading, science, writing, the arts, civics, economics, geography and U.S. history. NAEP does not provide scores for individual students or schools; instead, it offers results regarding subject-matter achievement, instructional experiences, and school environment for populations of students (e.g., fourth graders) and groups within those populations (e.g., female students, Hispanic students). NAEP results are based on a sample of student populations of interest." There are two different NAEP instruments, the Main and the Long-term Trend. For mathematics, the Main measures math content, including numeration, measurement, geometry, data analysis, statistics, and probability, and allows the use of calculators; the Long-term Trend measures a larger number of traditional arithmetic items and more sophisticated computational skills, without the use of calculators. According to Loveless, a senior scholar at the Brookings Institution and national commentator on issues in education, between 1990 and 2004 the Main and Long-term Trend tests agreed that students are gaining in mathematics but disagreed about the size of the increase. These discrepancies may indicate that the Trend scores are finally catching up with the huge gains reported on the Main in the 1990s (Loveless 2006).

There are at least two concerns about the NAEP. First, results may not be accurate because, from the perspective of students, this is a low-stakes test. Second, the NAEP is aligned with the NCTM mathematics standards, which traditionalist mathematicians and educators criticize. NAEP has responded that it has a long run of tests whose results are comparable to those of other instruments, implying that the NAEP has high validity.

In addition to these international and national tests, each state develops and administers its own tests which, since the passage of NCLB, have been used to determine AYP, adequate yearly progress. AYP is used to allocate federal funds and to impose sanctions on schools that show low performance. Each state test is tied to a set of state standards, which differ from state to state even though each state's standards may align in many ways with NCTM standards. The same is true of the definitions of proficiency which are also set by each state. NAEP appears to "set the bar" higher than many states (Loveless 2006), though students do better overall on state tests, perhaps because the state tests are the ones that have high stakes. These state tests are now being administered with increasing frequency. In the past, for example, Washington State tested at 4th, 7th, and 10th grade, and Oregon tested at 3rd, 5th, 8th, and 10th. Now there is mandatory testing of all students every year from 3rd through 8th grade, plus once in high school.

Obviously, there is no higher stake than having a school district's funding dependent on test results, and that stake has risen since some states require passing scores for the high school diploma. Mass Insight Education and Research Institute (April 2004) and Partnership for Learning (2007) have been studying Massachusetts and Washington since the late

1990s, describing these states as "two bellwether states of school reform," which are comparable for many reasons. Both states are "new economy states that made a substantial commitment to standards-based reform," they have similar demographics, and they have challenging exit exams for graduation from high school. There is a critical difference between the two states, however. Massachusetts targeted 2003 as the first year that high school diplomas would be dependent on achievement; in Washington this requirement was to have been implemented in 2008, but for math the date has now been put off until 2013.

Mass Insight's May 2004 report, "Lessons from the Front Lines of Standards-Based Reform: Four Benchmarks for an Effective State Program," states that in Massachusetts there was a large jump in scores when scores began to count, but that achievement in Washington has not climbed yet among 10th graders. The lessons learned in this study resulted in four recommended policies:

1. No double standards. Every student should be expected to meet challenging state standards.
2. State tests need to be aligned with standards and measure skills that really matter.
3. High school graduation exams should make achieve- ‧ment count.
4. Encourage schools to improve by linking funding to results.

The report also recommended that public funds should be invested in ways that help educators learn from each other. From the perspective of the four theses that drive the analysis presented in this book, these findings raise important and familiar questions. The emphasis is placed on student results on tests, and the motivators are threats of punishment. Students who fail will be denied diplomas, and schools that "fail" will be denied funding that might help them to improve. Schools that serve students who are poor or whose first language isn't English will be at a distinct disadvantage. Finally, these recommended policies do not speak to the expertise or the needs of teachers.

Educators who work with such state testing regimens face two additional frustrations. Districts and schools rarely receive assessment data in a timely fashion. For example, in Washington State the results of the WASL, the Washington Assessment of Student Learning, for the 2006–2007 academic year were released in late August 2007, leaving limited time for administrators or teachers to analyze student performance and plan changes to the curriculum or teaching methods. What is the value of annual testing if results are released too late to be used? Further, it is not clear that instruction in any state is well aligned with the content of these tests. According to the National Research Council's report of 2001, at that time there were few studies that examined the fit of tests to curricula. An earlier NRC report (1999), *Teaching, Testing, and Learning*, reinforces a well-known pedagogical truth. The most useful testing is regular, in the classroom, tied to individual students' progress, and related directly to what the teacher is presenting. Moreover, testing should use a variety of methods of assessment to get a full picture of what students are learning. Many teachers view state tests and other standardized instruments as less informative for teaching, and teachers also resent the time it takes to administer such tests. A common complaint in the classroom is that "All we ever do is test the kids. We don't have time to teach anymore." What educators want is for the resources put into testing to make a difference. So what will improve instruction?

Math Curricula

We have already surveyed the competing camps in the debate over the American versus the world math curriculum. In the United States, traditionalists and constructivists each promote instructional programs and materials that are aligned with their agenda and can point to test results that justify their positions and materials. An expanded description of the beliefs and practices associated with each camp (Smith 1993) explains the rationales for the different methods of instruction, curricula, and supporting technology.

Traditionalism

Traditionalists and back-to-basics advocates look for highly sequential instructional programs that emphasize arithmetic, the memorization of "math facts" at the elementary level, and such skills as algebraic operations and procedures, geometry with proofs, and related abstract applications at the middle and high school levels. This sequential approach is based on the belief that mathematics is an abstract and symbolic manipulation of quantitative information performed by operations on numbers. Teaching mathematics at the K–12 level from this perspective is designed to develop mental proficiency in numeric procedures. Because there are proven, effective and efficient techniques for learning mathematical reasoning and for doing computations, it follows that students who learn this way will be able to solve problems both quickly and accurately. The teacher's job is to transmit this knowledge and the necessary procedural skills. This style of pedagogy is rooted in behaviorist learning theory and is sometimes called a "teacher-centered" methodology, although the method has also been called "teacher-proof," because the delivery of the curriculum is so highly prescribed and sequenced that in the minds of some advocates, teachers do not need much training to deliver the material. Many parents who home-school their children use this approach because it seems to lend itself to independent learning. A key component of the method is repetitive practice. Teachers move through the textbook chapter by chapter to maintain the prescribed and preferred sequence of learning, although there are some "word problems" that require reasoning skills and that illustrate applications of what is learned.

Scholars such as Ball (1991, 2000, 2007) and Ma (1999), who have studied the pedagogical knowledge of excellent math teachers, provide evidence that the traditional method is flawed in that it places low value on a master teacher's skills for identifying common errors, developing concepts that many students can more easily learn, and generally facilitating the learning process. To put this another way, a completely mechanical application of the traditional teaching methods does not offer much help for students who just can't "get it," students for whom this abstract subject is inherently difficult.

A typical math lesson using this method, at almost any level of schooling, consists of reviewing the previous lesson; introducing and explaining the procedures to be learned next; assigning problems that students work on while the instructor monitors progress and intervenes to make sure that students are correctly applying techniques, and assigning problems that will be checked in the next class period. This describes the vast majority of U.S. mathematics classrooms. As the National Research Council states (NRC 2001), "mathematics teaching in the United States clearly has not changed a great deal in a century" (p. 50). This finding is important for two reasons, which we emphasize here. First, if math teaching has not really changed in a century, the various "new maths" have never really been implemented, because teachers were never trained to use them or to be comfortable with them. Second, the traditionalist camp is not in a strong position to claim that test scores are low because math teaching has been changed, because there has been no change at the roots of the system, down in the classroom. Scores may have dropped because school districts worked to keep a larger percentage of children in school, or because less time is being spent on math education because the curriculum has broadened to include other subjects, or for some other reason. Most Americans, young and old, have been instructed in the traditionalist manner, and many like this kind of math, because it is reassuring to have one way to find a correct answer and clear formulae to follow, even if we are not particularly adept at applying those techniques to the "real-world problems" of life.

It may be that people, particularly parents, are reacting to bad experiences in their or their childrens' math classes and don't think they should have to learn mathematics in new ways that they don't understand, but the almost religious fervor displayed by some of the most committed traditionalists appears to be generated by their certainty that this is the one right way to teach math and that any other way is wrong. Websites such as NYC HOLD (http://www.nychold.com) or Mathematically Correct (http://www.mathematicallycorrect. com) provide testimonies, some supported by research, about the effectiveness of instructional approaches built on the traditionalist philosophy of math education. The Saxon Math (http: //saxonpublishers.harcourtachieve.com/en-US/saxonmath_ home) textbooks are a good example of materials written from a traditionalist perspective. Indeed, many mathematicians and parents avidly attack practices that do not adhere to the traditionalist paradigm. As noted in the first chapter, traditionalists often observe that constructivist curricula do not assure that students learn enough of the basics to master any later approach to mathematics.

Schoenfeld (2004) describes how religious and political conservatives came to influence mathematics education in the 1970s, when an innovative National Science Foundation-supported elementary school science and social science curriculum met with initial success and then experienced a political backlash. The program was called "Man: A Course of Study," or MACOS. A Baptist minister objected to the content and approach of MACOS and initiated a media campaign that "claimed that the materials advocated sex education, evolution, a 'hippie-yippie philosophy,' pornography, gun control, and Communism" (Schoenfeld 2004, p. 260). The resulting public controversy led the NSF to conclude that it should not sponsor anything that might be viewed as a national curriculum. For math education, this meant that only a private organization, the National Council of Teachers of Mathematics, could step in and make national curricular recommendations.

The concern of traditionalist educators and parents about the lack of memorization in elementary-level math classes is similar to parental concern about phonics and whole-language approaches to reading. When traditionalists ask "where's the math?" they mean "where are the memorized multiplication tables and memorized formulae?" As we pointed out in the previous chapter, many constructivist programs, such as the Dutch Realistic Mathematics Education (RME), include this basic memorization. At the same time, it is true that some elementary teachers have been told that students should not be pushed to memorize math tables. Again, the qualities and qualifications of the teacher become the critical issue. How much does the teacher know about teaching math? How prepared is the teacher to help slow learners master basic material, to identify errors that students are making, to introduce other forms of math instruction, including memorization of multiplication tables, where the students need those skills? Where is the teacher?

Constructivism

Constructivism is the other main camp in what have been called the American math wars. Constructivist teaching is aligned with the NCTM standards and is the approach used by those who think math should be not only useful but should also make sense. Constructivist or reform-based math teachers want to promote conceptual understanding and meaning-making *along with* procedural knowledge and knowledge of math facts. Constructivists think it important to engage students in hands-on learning activities, often using physical models, simple sticks, and other objects, called manipulatives, and "real-life" applications to provide the context and motivation to learn math.

Mathematics teaching from this perspective is about locating contexts and setting up opportunities to develop the learners' knowledge and skills through their own actions, interactions, and mental abstractions. Contrary to what some traditionalists claim, learners are not asked to reinvent mathematics; rather, teachers structure appropriate activities and guide learners to acquire mathematical concepts and skills. This approach is "learner-centered" rather than "teacher-centered," and it calls for a high degree of sophistication from teachers, because the dialogue about solving a problem can take many more directions than a typical dialogue about how to understand a formula. For example, at the elementary level, a teacher might introduce numerical patterns by looking at the calendar or the clock; or use pennies, dimes, and dollars for modeling place value; or set up tables for learning about angles by building bridges.

Using a clock to teach basic numbers, rather than just learning the number system, presents interesting problems that may require more knowledge from a teacher than teaching the traditional way. Obviously a clock puts the numbers in order and provides a real-life example of the use of numbers. But a clock also introduces a number system based on 12, not 10. And on a clock, the answer to 12 + 1 is 1, not 13. Using pennies and dimes to indicate place value raises other problems. How can a dime be ten times the value of a penny when a dime is smaller than a penny? These examples are offered merely to show that for an elementary teacher, even teaching the simplest ideas about number requires anticipating these clever questions and responding with intelligent answers that can be grasped by very young learners.

Research showing the effectiveness of reform-based programs has been widely published and includes, among others, articles by Issacs, et al. (1997), Carroll (1998), Briars and Resnick (2000), and Riordan and Noyce (2001). The website for Mathematically Sane (http://www.mathematically-sane.com) includes a wealth of information by such authors as Van de Walle (2007), the author of the widely used textbook for aspiring teachers, *Elementary and Middle School Mathematics: Teaching Developmentally*. Warfield's assessment (Warfield April/May 2007) of the value of constructivist math can be found at http://www.math.washington.edu/~warfield/news/news139.html.

Boaler (2002) reported the results of one such study (an ethnographic case study) during the late 1990s that contrasted traditional and reform approaches to mathematics education at two English schools. Basing her conclusions on classroom observations, staff and student interviews, student assessments scores, and other credible evaluations, Boaler found that there was a measurable difference in the performance of the 13- to 16-year-old students whose cohorts she followed for three years. Boaler concluded that the reform-based school outperformed the traditional school on mathematics assessments. While the performance of students at the traditional school did somewhat better on the "purely procedural aspects," those at the reform-based school did much better on the "conceptual parts," and there was "no contest on tests of applications or problem-solving" as described by Schoenfeld (2002), who states in his preface that "Boaler's book thus provides some of the first comparative evidence that students who receive project-based instruction that does not focus on skills learn more—and different—mathematics than students receiving traditional skills-based instruction" (p. xi). Ball comments, on the cover of Boaler's book, "Boaler's compelling study provides a vivid portrait of contrasts in students' opportunities to learn in two dramatically different approaches to the curriculum and teaching of mathematics, supplying much-needed evidence about the teaching and learning of mathematics."

People who are well versed in constructivism and the approaches to instruction associated with it tend to believe that all people can become mathematically proficient; that learning mathematics is no more difficult than learning to read fluently and to write with facility; and that all Americans have the right to high-quality instruction that will allow them access to educational and economic prosperity. The latter belief is not really different from that of the traditionalists, but the means and methods of the two sides are substantially different, though there are also significant overlaps in content and pedagogy.

Curriculum and Textbooks

Right now, constructivist or reform-based math education, based on the NCTM Principles and Standards, is guiding much of the development of curricular materials in the United States. This is in spite of the fact that most math instruction in the classroom is still probably done in the traditionalist manner. One of the difficulties facing educational leaders is that they really do not know what approach is used within classrooms.

In Washington State, for example, there has been no study of what is actually happening in the classrooms, what texts have been adopted by school districts, how those texts are actually being used, and so on. Meanwhile, among advocates of one approach to math education or another, debate continues about different aspects of the curriculum.

When math educators discuss the format of a curriculum, they have in mind either a linear, sequential approach or what is called a spiral approach. In the spiral model, topics are taught and then revisited, so that students get an increasingly more sophisticated grasp of the skills and ideas. In the linear model, education begins with drill in basic facts and formulae, and then other skills are introduced. When higher math is introduced, a spiral model blends geometry, algebra, and trigonometry together, whereas on a strictly linear model, geometry is often taught independently of algebra and trigonometry. These distinctions are to some extent false, because trigonometry, for example, is by its very nature a combination of algebra and geometry.

There is a related debate about what is sometimes called the sequence of instruction. On a traditionalist model, students learn to count and recognize numerals in kindergarten, learn addition and subtraction to 20 in first grade, add and subtract to 100 in second grade, learn multi-digit operations in third grade, start division in fourth grade, and so on. Later, students are tracked into advanced or basic math classes. The reform-based model of education is similar, though more advanced concepts are generally presented earlier, as they are in European schools.

Increasingly, textbooks are supplemented by manipulatives, visual representations, models, and technological tools such as graphing calculators and software for computer modeling. The National Research Council's 2001 report *Adding It Up* states that "In 1996, teachers of 27% of the fourth graders in

NAEP reported that their students used counting blocks and geometric shapes at least once a week; 74% used them at least once a month; leaving 26% who seldom if ever used them. Teachers of 8% of the eighth graders said that their students used such manipulatives at least once a week, and teachers of more than half the students reported essentially no use" (p. 45). However, newer textbooks and instructional materials require more consistent and integrated use of physical models and manipulatives, along with technology software and the like, and publishers often provide workshops for teachers in such use when districts adopt new curriculum. Even with the availability of newer programs, however, there is scant evidence that a majority of teachers are integrating the hands-on materials into their instruction in ways intended by the developers. Without sufficient research regarding the fidelity of implementation of these new programs based on constructivism, we cannot say that teaching of mathematics has changed substantially. And, indeed, the TIMSS video study bears this out (Stigler and Hiebert 1997).

The Math Wars in the United States

In light of these characterizations of math education and the competing educational models, why has there been such intense conflict over math education? If the research shows that most teaching still follows a traditional model, how can traditionalists assert that any failures are caused by constructivism? If constructivist materials are adopted, but classroom instruction defaults to older methods of teaching, how can constructivists claim that the results of their programs are superior or different? If the comparisons to the achievement of other nations are deeply flawed, how can we know what is the underlying problem? And as we have observed repeatedly, where is the teacher and teacher preparation in this picture?

According to the Mathematics Learning Study Committee, sponsored by the National Academies of Sciences and Engineering, the Institute of Medicine, and the National Research Council in their 2001 report *Adding It Up*, "Apparently there has never been a time when U.S. students excelled in mathematics, even when schools enrolled a much smaller, more select portion of the population" (p. xiii). Obviously, our citizens have been dissatisfied with math education for a long time. The changes that launched the reforms started in the late 1970's with NCTM's *An Agenda for Action* (1980) and its proposals for ensuring that all students have access to mathematics instruction that fosters greater understanding. Opponents set out to put reformers on the defensive by asking parents to question any new methods. Schoenfeld, professor of education at the University of California, Berkeley, and at the time vice president of the U.S. National Academy of Education, offered his view of the conflict in 2004, when he wrote (Schoenfeld 2004, p. 254) that this "story is told from the perspective of a participant-observer who sits squarely in the middle of the territories claimed by both sides. I am a mathematician by training and inclination, hence, comfortable with the core mathematical values cherished by traditionalists. I have also . . . conducted research on mathematical thinking, learning, and teaching; I am thus equally at home with the 'process orientation' cherished by reformers." Schoenfeld continues, "An historical perspective reveals that the underlying issues being tested—Is mathematics for the elite or for the masses? Are there tensions between 'excellence' and 'equity?' Should mathematics be seen as a democratizing force or as a vehicle for maintaining the status quo?—are more than a century old . . ." Who gets to learn mathematics, and the nature of the mathematics that is learned, are matters of consequence.

This fact is one of the foundations of the math wars. It has been true for more than a century" (Schoenfeld 2004, pp. 253–4). Schoenfeld refers to Stanic's description (Stanic 1987) of the historic philosophical stances underpinning "the four perspectives on mathematics: (1) Humanists believed in 'mental discipline,' the ability to reason, and the cultural value of mathematics; (2) Developmentalists focused on the alignment of school curricula with the growing mental capacities of children; (3) Social efficiency educators thought of schools as the place to prepare students for their predetermined social roles; (4) Social meliorists (similar to those who believed in education for social mobility) focused on schools as potential sources of social justice" (Schoenfeld 2004, pp. 255–6). These competing forces have driven a competition over the authoring and adoption of textbooks, particularly by the largest states, such as California, Texas, and New York, where state boards make decisions for all schools. So a debate that is rooted in economic reality is played out through an economic competition over the sale of textbooks, where the decisions are made by state boards that may or may not include teachers.

Schoenfeld goes on to describe the combat in the State of California during the 1990s in these terms. The NCTM Standards were published in 1989, and the state adopted its own standards in 1992, building on the NCTM model. Textbook publishers had reform-based books available by 1993. The first cohort of students learned with these textbooks through the 1990s, with test data available at the turn of the century. "As it happens," Schoenfeld writes, "the evidence at this point is unambiguously in favor of reform . . . But such data turn out to be largely irrelevant to the story of the math wars. When things turn political, data really do not matter" (pp. 269–70). Things turned political in part because the new textbooks looked so different from the old ones. As Rosen (2000) summarized the problem: "The new textbooks were radically different from the traditional texts' orderly, sequential presentation of formulas and pages of practice problems familiar to parents. New texts featured colorful illustrations, assignments with lively, fun names, and sidebars discussing topics from the environment to Yoruba mathematics" (p. 61).

These conflicts, which have flared up in one state after another, have raised important questions. The conflicts have also deflected attention from what happens in the classroom. Reys, professor of mathematics education at the University of Missouri, Columbia, puts it this way: "I am tired of hearing from doomsday educational critics who would have us abandon new ideas and return to the "good old days"—particularly in math education, where American students fall way behind the rest of the world. Efforts to reform mathematics education are under way, but they have not reached many classrooms in the United States" (Reys 2002). Therefore, many researchers advocate for building a stronger research foundation to be able to work more effectively with the teachers who actually deliver the math curriculum. This is the finding of the RAND Mathematics Study Panel (2003), which published *Mathematical Proficiency for All Students: Toward a Strategic Research and Development Program in Mathematics Education*. Another group of math leaders gathered in 2004 to find common ground in the math wars (Ball, et al. 2005) and identified a set of principles on which they could agree:

1. Basic skills with numbers continue to be vitally important for everyday uses.
2. The ability to reason about and justify mathematical statements is fundamental, as is the ability to use terms and notation with appropriate degrees of precision.
3. Students must be able to formulate and solve problems. (p. 1056)

The group also agreed that students should have automatic recall of certain basic facts, should use calculators in a limited and appropriate way, should learn basic algorithms fluently, should master the basic operations with fractions, should learn how to solve real-world problems, should learn through a mixture of methods including exploration of ideas, and should be taught by teachers who know how to do all the math that they are teaching and also have skills in "how to reduce mathematical complexity and manage precision in ways that make the mathematics accessible to students while preserving its integrity" (pp. 1056–8). Once again, the last and most important words focus on that special ability that excellent math teachers have to illuminate complex ideas so that all students can grasp them.

Wu at the University of California, Berkeley, wrote that "Education seems to be plagued by false dichotomies . . . in mathematics education, this debate takes the form of 'basic skills or conceptual understanding'. . . . This bogus dichotomy would seem to arise from a common misconception of mathematics held by a segment of the public and the education community: that the demand for precision and fluency in the execution of basic skills in school mathematics runs counter to the acquisition of conceptual understanding. The truth is that in mathematics, skills and understanding are completely intertwined . . . In good art as in good mathematics, technique and conception go hand in hand" (Wu 1999, p.1).

A more subtle explanation for the math wars may be rooted in psychological phenomena that appear in any major cultural change, in this case the movement of the United States toward a K–12 math curriculum that would be appropriate for a society increasingly dependent on mathematical knowledge to keep up with technological progress. Both teachers and parents tend to want the next generation to learn as they did. Although states that introduced constructivist methods have offered teacher workshops, it takes a long time for the teachers themselves to re-learn mathematics in terms of the new models and to develop the vocabulary necessary to help students—and above all those students who have a hard time learning math—to comprehend math fully, not just as memorized facts and formulae, but also as a set of complex approaches to problem solving that makes the world more understandable. Elkind, author of *The Hurried Child* (2001), described how he pushed for the adoption of manipulatives in the classroom only to find that, instead of integrating them into instruction as meaningful representations of mathematics concepts, the teachers simply gave them to the students, who ultimately used the manipulatives to build "houses" or throw at each other (Elkind 1981), which turned out to be the same kind of problem that Norwegian teachers faced when they adopted a constructivist curriculum without adequate teacher preparation.

Stigler and Hiebert (1999) describe this problem in these words: "A problem in the U.S. approach to reform [is that] teachers can misinterpret reform and change surface features—for example, they include more group work; use more manipulatives, calculators, and real world problem scenarios; or include writing in the lesson—but fail to alter their basic approach to teaching mathematics" (pp. 106–7). The same researchers assert that "reform documents that focus teachers' attention on features of 'good teaching' in the absence of supporting contexts might actually divert attention away from the more important goals of student learning . . . they may inadvertently cause teachers to substitute the means for the ends—to define success in terms of specific features or activities instead of long-term improvement in learning" (pp. 107–8). As a result, the general public, as well as traditionalist mathematicians, may be led to believe that reform-based instruction is inferior, ineffective pedagogy. *This is truly the heart of the matter.* When traditionalist critics complain about teachers who adopt surface features of a new math program, some-times going so far as to postpone indefinitely the memoriza-tion of multiplication tables, the traditionalists are right that the new programs don't work—because they have never been implemented. When a master teacher at a top prep school, who has taught years of workshops at the Park City Math con-ference, explains the extraordinary power of constructivist methods when they are well applied, of course he or she is right—but many teachers do not have that level of knowledge either of math or about the teaching of math.

Does mathematics teaching and learning have to be either/or: traditional or reform-based? Can't it be both/and? Many think so. Yet without a critical mass of teachers skillfully teach-ing in a both/and model and students clearly demonstrating that the goals of the reform-based movement in mathematics education have been realized, few educators have the energy and will to sustain the effort. It is important to keep in mind that just returning to full traditionalism, with teachers drilling students, may not be an appropriate fallback position, because the American experience indicates that while that approach serves bright and gifted kids well, it will always leave others without a good grasp of math. (See, for example, NCTM 2000).

What then does it take for teachers to successfully instruct their students so that they are able to demonstrate high pro-ficiency in the skills and knowledge that are rated on cred-ible international comparisons that examine truly comparable groups of students? Mathematicians and mathematics educa-tors, who do not always communicate, agree that "teachers' mathematical knowledge must be developed through solid initial teacher preparation and ongoing, systematic profes-sional learning opportunities" (Ball et al. 2005, p. 1058).

Teacher Knowledge of Math

According to the research reported in *Education Week* (2007) "the specific characteristics that constitute an effective teacher are hotly debated." There is, however, widespread agreement that teacher quality matters; "in fact," according to Rice (2003), "it is the most important school-related factor influencing student achievement," a point re-iterated by the American Federation of Teachers (2007): "Research findings demonstrate that teacher quality is the single most important variable affecting student achievement." Citations of this kind can be multiplied (see the 2007 Center for Teaching Quality report, "What We Know," for example). Yet there is disagreement about what teacher quality is, exactly, and how to measure it. As we have argued, this is not a question that can be approached simply in the abstract. While the definition of general teacher quality is important, what we need to understand better in both the United States and the world is what makes a good math teacher. The National Center for Education Statistics notes the important distinction between teacher preparation, on the one hand, and teacher practices, on the other (NCES 1999b).

The Economic Policy Institute (2007) names five broad categories of measurable and policy-relevant indicators of teacher quality, although there appear to be differences among the criteria most important for elementary as compared to high school teachers. These indicators are teacher experience, teacher preparation programs, teacher certification, teacher coursework, and teachers' own test scores. Advanced degrees in the teaching subject area, as opposed to degrees in education, have a greater impact at the high school than at the elementary level. A mathematics certificate or endorsement is particularly important at the high school level. Content coursework is important, as is coursework in pedagogy.

Finally, teacher test scores that show high verbal ability are associated with higher levels of student achievement, though test scores that measure basic content and teaching skills are less consistent predictors of teacher and student performance. One may therefore hypothesize that really good math teachers are people who have good content knowledge, good pedagogical training, good analytical thinking skills, and the verbal skills to describe, develop, and explain mathematical concepts at the students' levels of understanding.

Teacher training programs are accredited by professional accrediting organizations, such as the National Council for Accreditation of Teacher Education (NCATE). Teachers in training complete extensive practica and pass both content exams and tests of their pedagogical skills. Teachers are then hired and assessed by districts. Some districts have a wide choice of applicants and can be choosy, but most have difficulty filling positions with well-prepared, experienced mathematics teachers. Schools provide extensive opportunities for learning on the job, and there is frequent evaluation of teachers' performance, with a dynamic tension about evaluation that plays out among administrators, school boards, parents' associations, and teachers' associations. About half of America's teachers have earned masters' degrees (NCES, January 1999). Continuing professional development classes are required for continued licensure. Unfortunately, much of the continuing education of teachers is performed in a traditional "sit and get" approach, even when the objective is to help teachers learn other techniques of teaching such as those encouraged by constructivist teaching models. Teachers often complain about the quality of in-service classes, and in the case of training in new textbooks, the trainers are often not teachers themselves but representatives of textbook companies.

Additional options for teacher development include National

Board Certification (National Board for Professional Teaching Standards, 2008), graduate degrees and coursework, and other experiences, such as Math-Science Partnerships, regional "Math Learning Center" classes, and "Math Academies" such as the Center for Mathematics and Science Education at the University of Wisconsin and the Park City Math Conferences, all of which provide teachers with various opportunities for mastering math and teaching skills. WestEd is "a non-profit, research agency with a staff of over 500 educators located in 16 offices throughout the country" that offers "Math Matters, a comprehensive, long term development program" (www.wested.org). Math educator Marilyn Burns runs math workshops of a similar kind (Math Solutions Professional Development, 2008). Ruth Parker's Mathematics Education Collaborative (Mathematics Education Collaborative, 2008) and Kathy Richardson's Math Perspectives Teacher Development Center (Math Perspectives, 2008), located in Washington State, operate workshops in many states. What one can conclude from the presence of such resources is that many committed people have been working to improve the content and teaching knowledge of math teachers and that many of these programs aim to supplement whatever is provided in traditional teacher education programs and teacher in-service programs. The existence of these programs is evidence of the problem as well as the many creative solutions available across the nation right now. Without offering an exhaustive content analysis of what these programs teach, it is possible nevertheless to observe that, while these programs touch upon some of the same issues, they also can take different perspectives. Some focus more on mastering math, others on pedagogical knowledge. The work of scholars such as Deborah Ball would suggest that while such programs may contribute a great deal to the quality of American math education, we need to know still more in order to offer better teacher education in mathematics.

One relatively new approach to helping teachers is the idea of employing math "coaches" to support both teachers and students in the classroom. The role of these instructional coaches varies, but it usually includes professional development, ensuring that district-mandated curricula are used, and sometimes working with students in the manner of math tutors. Because math coaches are sometimes hired from pools of math graduates who do not necessarily have extensive experience as teachers or specialized knowledge about the teaching of mathematics itself, these programs have had mixed results in various districts. A paper titled "Math Coaching in Boston" (Center for Leadership and Learning Communities 2005) states that "it is increasingly apparent that math coaches need to develop a specialized kind of knowledge—knowledge that is distinctly different than the pedagogical content knowledge coaches developed as classroom teachers—in order to effectively support mathematics leadership development in schools."

Two issues are confounded here. Math teaching is not the same as leadership in mathematics curriculum and instruction. It also appears that the specialized math teaching knowledge is similar to that at the heart of Ball's and Ma's research. A selection of job and program descriptions from California and Washington (see, for example, Silicon Valley Mathematics Initiative (2006) and Smaller Learning Communities (2006)) underlines this reality. These programs discuss methods for increasing teacher content knowledge and for building communities of math teachers. The Silicon Valley program speaks of coaches who can help teachers understand student thinking about math, though it is not clear where the coaches get this knowledge, where it is reported in the literature, or how they are selected for these roles. Of course, coaches without extensive teacher training may be very helpful to teachers who are teaching outside their areas of study, as in the case of many elementary teachers who do not have extensive backgrounds in mathematics or in the case of middle grades teachers who may be assigned to teach basic math when their training is in a different field of study. Holmes and Ingersoll (Holmes Group, 1986) discuss the problem of "out of field" teaching. This issue is important enough to deserve additional attention.

Teaching Mathematics

Across the United States, there are different expectations for math teachers at different levels of schooling. At all levels, instruction is grounded in at least one of the competing learning theories. At the elementary level, all American teachers teach mathematics, and there are few, if any, specific requirements for math endorsements. People who choose to teach at the elementary level are rarely proficient mathematicians, although some come from subject fields or work experiences that are math-intensive. Some elementary and early childhood-level educators have specialized in math education. These teachers seek to become experts in how children learn mathematics and develop strategies and methods for effectively instructing our youngest learners. However, it is widely documented that most elementary and many middle-school teachers do not have the math content knowledge that their secondary colleagues must demonstrate through the courses and assessments they take as part of their endorsement. Under NCLB, to be considered "highly qualified," teachers whose primary responsibility is math (secondary-level teachers for the most part) must have a bachelor's degree and full state certification or licensure and must prove that they know each subject that they teach through a demonstration of competence (i.e., a major or equivalent coursework in math, passage of a state-developed test such as Praxis II that assesses content knowledge, etc.). However, the focus is on content, not pedagogy or instructional effectiveness. Many high school teachers, of course, do not have this "highly qualified" standing, because there is a significant shortage of math and science teachers at American secondary schools. The NRC 2001 report, *Adding It Up*, shows, as well, that U.S. elementary and middle school teachers have a limited knowledge of math, including the math they teach. Altogether, it appears that American children stand a high chance of learning the most basic mathematical ideas, which require a new kind of abstract thinking, from teachers who are not well prepared to convey this information and this type of conceptualizing.

We have mentioned Ma's work previously. Schoenfeld called Ma's book, *Knowing and Teaching Elementary Mathematics* (Ma 1999), "an underground hit, perhaps the only manuscript I know that has the attention and favor of both sides of the 'math wars'" (Schoenfeld 2004). Ma's study compared the responses of U.S. and Chinese elementary teachers to questions about how they would present four kinds of problems: subtraction with regrouping, multi-digit multiplication, division by fractions, and area and perimeter. What Ma found is both shocking and compelling. Although the American teachers, who were considered above average math teachers, demonstrated a method for solving the problems and teaching their students how to calculate correct answers, these teachers' arithmetic knowledge was procedural and shallow compared to that of their Chinese counterparts. The Chinese teachers, for example, did not merely instruct students to "borrow" in subtraction, but used the opportunity to explain place value. In division by fractions, "only one among the 23 U.S. teachers generated a conceptually correct representation," while "90% of the Chinese teachers" could explain what division by fractions meant.

Moreover, all of the Chinese teachers could calculate a correct answer to the problem 1¾ divided by ½, while only 40% of the American teachers could. When the teachers were asked to tell a story to illustrate this problem, only one American teacher, but over 90% of the Chinese teachers, could do so.

Ma did not set out to discredit American teachers but wanted to find out what was behind the differences in teaching and learning math that she saw in her experiences as an educator in both countries. Ma was perplexed about why well-educated American teachers performed differently from their Chinese counterparts. She discovered that Chinese teachers begin their teaching careers with a better understanding of basic math. Moreover, their understanding was more coherent, and they systematically used a mathematical vocabulary. Ma summarized her findings by commenting that "Although U.S. teachers were concerned with teaching for conceptual understanding, their responses reflected a view common in the United States—that elementary mathematics is 'basic,' an arbitrary collection of facts and rules in which doing mathematics means following set procedures step-by-step to arrive at answers" (Ma 1999, quoting Ball 1991). So what kind of knowledge do math teachers need?

Three Essential Bodies of Knowledge

For the last two decades, Ball and her colleagues at the University of Michigan, and others, have tried to work out in detail the kind of knowledge math teachers need to be effective. The NRC report *Adding It Up* (2001) offered this definition of the categories of knowledge: "Although we have used the term knowledge throughout, we do not mean it exclusively in the sense of knowing about. Teachers must also know how to use their knowledge in practice. Teachers' knowledge is of value only if they can apply it to their teaching: it cannot be divorced from practice" (pp. 379–80). So there is knowing about math, knowing how students learn math, and knowing how to apply math in teaching, or how to teach math. Each of these is worth specifying in some detail.

Knowing About Math

Knowledge of mathematics itself includes knowledge of mathematical facts, concepts, procedures, and the relationships among them; knowledge of the ways that mathematical ideas can be represented; and knowledge of mathematics as a discipline—in particular, how mathematical knowledge is produced, the nature of discourse in mathematics, and the norms and standards of evidence that guide argument and proof. According to Ma (1999), profound understanding of fundamental mathematics is defined as "an understanding of the terrain of fundamental mathematics that is deep, broad, and thorough . . . Teachers with this deep, vast and thorough understanding do not invent connections between and among mathematical ideas, but reveal and represent them in terms of mathematics teaching and learning" (p. 120). Such teaching and learning tends to have the following four properties: "1) Connectedness—a teacher makes connections among mathematical concepts and procedures . . . this intention will prevent students' learning from being fragmented. Instead of learning isolated topics, students will learn a unified body of knowledge. 2) Multiple perspectives—teachers appreciate and provide mathematical explanations for different facets of an idea and various approaches to a solution. 3) Basic ideas—teachers display mathematical attitudes and are aware of 'simple but powerful basic concepts and principles of mathematics,' and they revisit and reinforce these basic ideas. 4) Longitudinal coherence—teachers are not limited to the knowledge that should be taught in a certain grade; they have a fundamental understanding of the whole elementary math curriculum" (p.

122). While some of these descriptions need to be enriched with examples, Ma's idea of a good math teacher seems to be someone who knows the whole K–12 math curriculum and its applications so well that she or he can readily help students to see relevance, connections, and multiple ways to approach every problem, so that every student, no matter her ability or interest, can learn the fundamentals well. This leads to the second form of knowledge.

Knowing How Students Learn Math

Teachers' knowledge of their students and how children learn mathematics must allow them to grasp how each child understands math and then project that student's trajectory of learning math. Researchers have gained an extensive, though still incomplete, knowledge about how students' mathematical thinking develops over time. Many elementary and middle school teachers pass on their own misconceptions. A method called Cognitively Guided Instruction (CGI) attempts to address this problem by modeling teaching on what is known about children's thinking. "Our engagement with teachers is driven by two principles," Carpenter et al. (2000) write of this method: "1) we focus interactions with teachers on the fundamental ideas underlying the development of children's thinking about mathematics, and 2) we build on the teachers' existing knowledge" (p. 2). This same group of researchers found that while many teachers have a deep intuitive knowledge of how students think about math, because the teachers' knowledge is fragmented, they do not always use that body of knowledge in their teaching. In CGI training, teachers learn how to interpret their students' actions and questions so that students can be guided with questions that build students' skills. Many textbooks and teacher training programs are grappling with the problem of math instruction at this level, though much more needs to be known about how students learn, and more teachers need to be introduced to this knowledge. It is not yet clear that teachers can just learn the methods without first having the deep mathematical knowledge of which Ma speaks.

Knowing How to Teach Math

Math teachers must also understand good instructional practices—an expertise that demands both good knowledge of math and a well-honed understanding of how students learn this abstract subject. This practical knowledge includes the mandated curriculum itself and classroom teaching practices. In some cases, teachers do not understand what might be called the overall shape of the new curricula and textbooks that are chosen by textbook committees. Without a good understanding of the overall design of a curriculum, it is hard to teach the parts, and this may explain why many teachers default to the curriculum they learned as students, disregarding what is in the texts. And that, in turn, explains why some districts use math coaches simply to introduce and explain the curriculum and the textbooks, rather than to grapple with deeper issues of mathematics and math teaching. The NRC report *Adding It Up* (p. 380) specifies the following interrelated components that characterize proficient math teaching:

1. Conceptual understanding of the core knowledge required in the practice of teaching,
2. Fluency in carrying out basic instructional routines,
3. Strategic competence in planning effective instruction and solving problems that arise during instruction,
4. Adaptive reasoning in justifying and explaining one's instructional practices and in reflecting on those practices so as to improve them,
5. Productive disposition toward mathematics, teaching, learning, and the improvement of practice.

In their similar research study, "Effects of Teachers' Mathematical Knowledge for Teaching on Student Achievement" (Hill et al. 2005), Hill and her colleagues looked at two ways of assessing teaching knowledge. Their basic finding, as we have stated earlier, is that teacher competence does not correlate well with basic teacher "resources" such as the number of college courses in math they took, or the number of degrees they earn, or their ability to ace math tests. Rather, it was "process-product" knowledge that was more important, and this seems to correlate with a different set of teachers' intellectual skills of the kind that are described, for example, in the NRC report (2001) category that includes "adaptive reasoning," or the kind of creative problem solving that teachers use when faced with students who don't understand. In light of these findings about the difficulties of teaching math well and the three distinct kinds of knowledge teachers must have, how is America to go about improving math instruction so that all students can master math at least to some degree? How does the nation meet the NCTM goal of educational equity in mathematics education?

Improving Math Instruction

What needs to change to improve American math instruction? What the debate over international tests and competing theories of education has taught us is just this: we need to discount what the tests say, because they are based on faulty comparisons, and we need to back away from the belief that the solution lies in a particular pedagogical theory and its associated textbooks. It appears that the quality of math education needs to be measured first of all in terms of the three kinds of knowledge that teachers must possess to be effective: deep knowledge of mathematics itself (content knowledge), good knowledge of learning math (pedagogical knowledge), and finally a specialized knowledge of how to help students understand the sometimes difficult abstractions of mathematical reasoning (pedagogical content knowledge). If we are to overcome the prejudice that math is an inherently difficult subject that many people will never understand, then we must believe that there are gifted or experienced teachers who have learned ways of engaging learners in numerical ideas so that the majority of their students understand them. The research to date indicates that we have not yet developed a sufficiently comprehensive knowledge of these skills to be able to train math teachers to be uniformly excellent, although enough knowledge is available that good programs of teacher training and in-service education can be offered.

Ma (1999) puts the issue this way, with a slightly different emphasis: "Having considered teachers' knowledge of school mathematics in depth, I suggest that to improve mathematics education for students, an important action that should be taken is improving the quality of their teachers' knowledge of mathematics . . . Given that the parallel of the two gaps is not mere coincidence, it follows that while we want to work on improving students' mathematics education, we also need to improve their teachers' knowledge of school mathematics" (p. 144). Ma offers several additional recommendations: 1) Enhance the interaction between teachers' study of school mathematics and how to teach it. This means, among other tasks, helping teachers to overcome the belief that elementary mathematics is basic, superficial, and commonly [that is, easily] understood. Ma argues that elementary mathematics are far more complex and offer an opportunity both to introduce a rigorous mathematical vocabulary and to lay down a foundation of understanding on which later math can be built. 2) Refocus teacher preparation so that teachers are given both comprehensive training in mathematics and also instruction in how to teach math effectively. At this time, many education students take a course in the teaching of mathematics that offers pedagogical strategies but assumes that the students have an adequate grasp of the underlying mathematics. 3) Understand the role that curricular materials, including text-books and manipulatives, might play in reform. When new curricula are introduced, school districts have an opportunity, as well as a duty, to assure that the new approaches are well understood and that teachers have an adequate understanding of the math itself. 4) Understand that the key to reform is a focus on substantial mathematics, or what Ma has called a profound understanding of mathematics.

The NRC takes a somewhat more forceful position, contending that

> "school mathematics education of yesterday, which had a practical basis, is no longer viable. Rote learning of arithmetic procedures no longer has the clear value it once had. . . . Too few U.S. students leave elementary and middle school with adequate mathematical knowledge, skill and confidence. . . . Widespread failure to learn mathematics limits individual possibilities and hampers national growth" (National Research Council 2001, p. 407).

National growth is of course a practical matter, so it is not clear in what sense practical math is no longer viable. However, NRC offers these recommendations to improve math education (summarized from p. 410):

1. Instruction should not be based on extreme positions that students learn, on the one hand, solely by internalizing what a teacher or book says or, on the other hand, solely by inventing mathematics on their own.
2. Teachers' professional development should be high in quality, sustained, and systematically designed and

deployed to help all students develop mathematical proficiency. Schools should support, as a central part of teachers' work, engagement in sustained efforts to improve their mathematics instruction. This support requires the provision of time and resources.

3. The coordination of curriculum, instructional materials, assessment, instruction, professional development, and school organization around the development of mathematical proficiency should drive school improvement efforts.

4. Efforts to improve students' learning should be informed by continued research into the learning of mathematics.

The NRC concludes that

"No country—not even those performing highest on international surveys of mathematics achievement—has attained the goal of mathematical proficiency for all students. It is an extremely ambitious goal, and the United States will never reach it by continuing to tinker with the controls of educational policy, pushing one button at a time. . . . Coordinated, systemic, and sustained modifications will need to be made in how school mathematics instruction has commonly proceeded, and support of new and different kinds will be required. Leadership and attention to the teaching of mathematics are needed in the formulation and implementation of policies at all levels of the educational system" (p. 432).

Stigler and Hiebert, in their book *The Teaching Gap* (1999), say that "although most popular U.S. reform efforts have avoided a direct focus on teaching, there are some notable exceptions. One of these has been in the domain of mathematics, where the NCTM has made a strong effort to improve classroom mathematics teaching" (p. 104). They cite the

NCTM *Professional Standards for Teaching Mathematics* (1991), but at the same time, they conclude that the TIMSS video studies of math teaching show far more effective teaching in Japanese than in American schools. Moreover, the TIMSS data suggest that the Japanese have a more effective approach to improving the performance of math teachers by focusing on the improvement of each specific math lesson. "The premise behind lesson study is simple," they write. "If you want to improve teaching, the most effective place to do so is in the context of the classroom lesson" (Stigler and Hiebert 1999, p. 111). Their conclusion, in other words, goes beyond what Ball and Ma have suggested in this sense. The focus should be on working to increase teachers' comprehension of math and ability to teach math, but the method for achieving the improvement should begin with learning experiences that help teachers improve their presentation of specific lessons.

Stigler and Hiebert write about a Lesson Study process that includes the following steps: 1) defining the problem, 2) planning the lesson, 3) teaching the lesson, 4) evaluating the lesson and reflecting on its effect, 5) revising the lesson, 6) teaching the revised lesson, 7) evaluating and reflecting again, and 8) sharing the results. All of this must be done by teachers working together in a collaborative manner, which is the best practice of Chinese teachers, as Ma found. Such a program of improvement might involve outside educators and consultants, but much of the work must be done through math teachers in schools and districts working together, in a non-judgmental way, to hone each other's skills. In China, of course, teachers have the advantage that they teach only math.

Stigler and Hiebert believe this kind of regimen will work to reform mathematics teaching because lesson study is a long-term, continuous improvement model, it maintains a constant focus on direct improvement of teaching in context, and it is collaborative. Teachers who participate in lesson study see themselves contributing to the development of knowledge about teaching as well as to their own professional skill. "In Japan," they write, "educators can look back over the past fifty years and believe that teaching has improved. In the United States, we cannot do this. We can see fashions and trends, ups and downs. But we cannot see the kind of gradual improvement that marks true professions. . . . We must take the first step toward building a system that will, over time, lead to improvement of teaching and learning in the American class. We need new ideas for teaching, ideas such as those provided by videos from Japan and Germany. But instead of copying these ideas, we must feed them into our own research and development system for improvement of classroom teaching. And we must empower teachers to be leaders in this process" (Stigler and Hiebert 1999, p. 127).

The National Mathematics Advisory Panel Final Report 2008

In response to the ongoing concern about mediocre student performance and the apparently never-ending battle over the "right" approach to learning and teaching math, President George W. Bush created the National Mathematics Advisory Panel (NMAP) in April 2006 and charged it to "advise the President and the Secretary [of Education] on ways to 'foster greater knowledge of and improved performance in mathematics among American students . . . with respect to the conduct, evaluation, and effective use of the results of research relating to proven-effective and evidence-based mathematics instruction'" (National Math Advisory Panel 2008, p. 7). The findings and recommendations of the NMAP concur with our own review of the national and international literature on mathematics education and lend credence to the four critical insights we have presented, insights that may explain what isn't happening or what needs to change in order to realize the hopes and expectations of math reformers.

The Panel agrees that "the delivery system in mathematics education—the system that translates mathematical knowledge into value and ability for the next generation—is broken and it must be fixed" (p. 11). They contend that the essence of their findings is to "put first things first" (p. 11) meaning that: 1) the PreK–8 mathematics curriculum should be streamlined and emphasize critical topics in the early grades; 2) math instruction should be based on "what is clearly known from rigorous research about how children learn" (p. 11), including providing a strong start from the first years of schooling; recognizing the mutually reinforcing benefits of conceptual understanding, procedural fluency, and automatic recall of facts; and recognizing that effort, not just inherent talent, counts in mathematical achievement; 3) mathematically knowledgeable classroom teachers have a central role in math education and should be hired, trained, and evaluated based on their demonstration of effective teaching; 4) instruction should be designed and practiced based on high-quality research and professional judgment of classroom teachers, and should not be either entirely "student-centered or teacher-directed" but an appropriate combination of both under specific conditions; 5) national and state assessments should be improved to reflect increased emphasis on "the most critical knowledge and skills leading to Algebra" (p. 12); and 6) the nation must build its capacity for rigorous research and application to inform policy and practice more effectively, stating that the Panel found little or insufficient research "relating to a great many matters of concern . . ." Finally, the Panel stated that "This journey, like that of the post-Sputnik era, will require a commitment to "learning as we go along"" (p. 13).

The NMAP report begins by claiming that "without sub-stantial and sustained changes to its educational system, the United States will relinquish its leadership in the 21st century" (p. xi) and that "there are large, persistent disparities in math-ematics achievement related to race and income—disparities that are not only devastating for individuals and families but also project poorly for the nation's future" (p. xii). It con-cludes by saying that "No longer can we accept that a rigorous mathematics education is reserved for the few who will go on to be engineers or scientists. Mathematics may indeed be 'the new literacy'; at the least, it is essential for any citizen who is to be prepared for the future." The Panel addresses what it sees as major obstacles to resolving the math wars in the U.S. by saying that "this is not a conclusion about any single ele-ment of the system. It is about how the many parts do not now work together to achieve a result worthy of this country's values and ambitions" and that "Debates regarding the rela-tive importance of . . . aspects of mathematical knowledge are misguided . . . These capabilities are mutually supportive, each facilitating the learning of the other" (p. xiii).

It is apparent that the Panel's conclusions and recommenda-tions are strongly aligned with what many see as the tradition-alist viewpoint. A publisher of math textbooks and software is quoted saying "This report is biased in favor of teaching arithmetic and not [modern] mathematics . . . and it's biased in favor of procedures and not applied skill." A spokesperson from NCTM said that "the report brings 'unprecedented focus' to math instruction and addresses many of the actions needed to improve math education" but that "while many panel rec-ommendations 'are supported by high-quality research, others extend beyond the report's reach'" (Cavanaugh 2008a). Edu-cators, schools, and vendors are responding to the NMAP report, and it is having a major influence on the development and selection of instructional materials, with special emphasis on getting more students capable and confident with algebraic concepts and skills at the elementary level and bridging the gap to middle school and beyond (Cavanaugh 2008b).

Perhaps one of the most important findings of the NMAP research is that the "essential qualities of math teaching remain unknown," a major conclusion of our own research and study of math education. A real transformation of mathematics education, of the scope being called for in this country, would be dependent on pervasive, effective, differentiated instruction from the earliest years of schooling, designed, presented, and managed by a highly qualified, mathematically proficient workforce of educators at the pre-school through graduate levels of college. Deborah Ball, an NMAP member who chaired its working group on teacher issues, concurred that many of the Panel's conclusions about improving teaching are tentative because enough high-quality research has not yet been done, and she stated, "We should put a lot of careful effort over the next decade into this issue so that we can be in a much different place 10 years from now" (Cavanaugh 2008c).

Who Is Responsible for Reform?

If better instruction by more knowledgeable and skillful teachers will lead to better learning in America, who must take responsibility for the needed changes? From a policy perspective, the responsibility is divided among all the stakeholders. Schools of education must examine the criteria for selecting future teachers with an eye to the importance of mathematical aptitude. Math education classes must involve profound mathematics, lesson study, and learning about research concerning how students learn math. State certification requirements must mandate these kinds of changes in teacher education programs. Districts that hire and continually educate professional teachers must think of creating dedicated math teaching positions and providing the time necessary for collaborative work groups of teachers to engage in the constant improvement that is characteristic of Chinese and Japanese teachers. Foundations and government agencies must fund additional research into the kind of work that Ball, Ma, and many others have been doing to understand the specialized knowledge of excellent math teachers. The public can help by supporting teachers as they endeavor to master more mathematics, to learn how to help students who have difficulty learning math, and to establish the formal and informal communication networks that will support lesson study and the development of excellent, specialized math teaching skills.

As Stigler and Hiebert and others have argued, teaching is a cultural activity. The culture of math education in America needs to change, but cultural change must come gradually to be meaningful and lasting. American thinking about math education, we have found, has been sidetracked by attention to international test results and an internal debate over traditionalism and constructivism. It may be a more fruitful strategy to invest time and resources instead on measures that will help teachers to master the three kinds of knowledge they need: knowledge of math, knowledge of learning math, and knowledge above all about the best way to engage all learners in meaningful mathematics learning, especially those students for whom math is hard. We turn next to what research tells us about the state of mathematics education in Washington State. Washington State is not extremely different from the rest of the United States, although it presents its own unique mix of issues.

3

Math Education in Washington State

An Overview of State Reform Issues

Now we turn our focus from global and national to Washington State. Washington State began an important cycle of work on math education with the 1993 Washington State Reform Law (House Bill 1209), which set in place expectations that math teaching (along with other subject areas) would move from a "teacher-centered" process to a "student-centered" educational environment. The Superintendent of Public Instruction served as the executive director of the Commission on Student Learning, which set out to determine the essential knowledge and skills that students would need to contribute to the economic future of Washington State.

The Commission created the Washington Assessment of Student Learning (WASL) to monitor progress with respect to the Essential Academic Learning Requirements (EALRs), also called the Washington State Learning Standards, which provide an overview of what students should know and be able to do in grades K–12. These standards were further defined through the Grade Level Expectations (GLEs), which provide detail about what students should know and be able to do at each grade level. Students demonstrate where they are along the learning continuum toward meeting subject area standards by their performance on the WASL.

By 1996, the state had begun to implement the WASL to

measure these essential skills. Meanwhile, the legislature introduced an accountability law that would have imposed sanctions on schools that did not carry out reforms and demonstrate appropriate student achievement. While such laws passed at the federal level and in other states, the law failed in the Washington State Legislature. Instead, the legislature funded the Office of Superintendent of Public Instruction (OSPI) to develop a process to support schools as they undertook necessary reforms.[1]

Since the WASL was meant to be the "floor" for achievement rather than the aspiration, the state set out to accomplish the following three tasks in order to reach this minimum goal: 1) students needed to have curricula aligned with the EALRs; 2) students needed to take higher levels of math, including geometry and at least some trigonometry, by the end of the first semester of the sophomore year; and 3) instruction needed to be aligned with these goals. The Commission on Student Learning was suspended in 1999 after it had written the EALRs, developed the WASL, and designed a support system to improve student achievement, focusing on higher standards and reliable assessment of student performance (Commission on Student Learning, 1994).

These were meaningful changes in the way Washington schools operated. However, the reform efforts focused primarily on curriculum and standards. Our research indicates that these kinds of reform efforts by themselves may not produce substantial changes in instructional methods, nor do they develop the mathematical skills and knowledge in the teaching force that are needed to foster the intra-individual as well as institutional transformations required for "second-order" changes.

---

1. Part of the Budget Proviso for the 2002 education legislation, Washington State.

Improvement Efforts in Washington

Washington is not without well-intentioned efforts to address its problems in mathematics education. According to the Washington Association of Colleges for Teacher Education (WACTE), "Most WACTE member schools are engaged in cutting-edge research and field work." "Improving Success in Mathematics: Research and Projects Underway in the State of Washington" (WACTE, November 2006) cites work being done at the University of Washington (UW), Evergreen State College (ESC), Eastern Washington University (EWU), and Washington State University (WSU). Several themes emerge from this document:

1) *Revamping math programs.* A National Science Foundation grant to the UW Department of Mathematics, in conjunction with UW College of Education professors Ilana Horn and Jim King, provides funding to help high school teachers revamp their math programs, adopt new interactive curricula focused on problem-solving, and change their methods of teaching. Researchers found that "working collaboratively, instead of isolated within their own classrooms, helped [teachers] more effectively hone curriculum and teaching methods to students' needs" (WACTE 2006, p. 3). They reported that "by year's end, changes in the first-year math classrooms were dramatic. Students were engaged, and they were engaged in higher-level math thinking" (p. 4), and one veteran classroom teacher stated "This is by far the most growth I've ever made as a professional" (p. 4).

2) *Developing teacher knowledge.* Faculty members in the Master In Teaching (MIT) program at Evergreen State College are partnering with a middle school to "support the

enriched math curriculum through consultation as well as placing practicum students and student teachers in this program" (p. 4); and Anita Lenges at ESC, through a UW grant, is working collaboratively "with mathematics and math education faculty across the state to learn what is the mathematics knowledge needed for teachers to teach mathematics" (p. 4). There are several projects at EWU with both pre-service and in-service math teachers, including professional development opportunities such as a project with Partners in Learning (PiL), the grant-funded collaboration between EWU and Cheney School District. At WSU, Amy Roth McDuffie has been conducting research "on the professional development of pre-service and practicing teachers in mathematics education . . . [focusing] on professional growth toward more student-centered approaches." McDuffie describes her research in journal articles such as "Mathematics Teaching as a Deliberate Practice: An Investigation of Elementary Pre-service Teachers; Reflective Thinking during Student Teaching" (McDuffie 2004) and "The Teacher as Researcher" (McDuffie 2005).

3) *University-school partnerships.* A large intervention called the Mathematics Case Study Project is a partnership among three universities—EWU, WSU, and UW—and "seven high-needs districts throughout the state" that work together to "improve teacher understanding of mathematics content, standards, teaching practice; foster a culture of teacher leadership; and provide teachers and school with materials specially designed to link instruction to GLEs" (Mathematics Case Study Project). Another project—Partnership for Reform in Secondary Science and Mathematics (PRiSSM—is funded by the Washington Office of the Superintendent of Public Instruction (OSPI)

through the federal Mathematics/Science Partnership Program, working out of the Educational Service District and WSU in Vancouver, WA. In this three-year project, PLCs (professional learning communities) are established in schools for grades 6–12 math and science teachers, with the goal of providing long-term professional development that leads to "conceptual and applicable student learning" that targets "increasing leadership capacity in individual buildings and strengthening the understanding and implementation of high quality teaching. . . . The bulk of the professional development occurs during ongoing PLC meetings as teachers, supported by a Facilitator, engage in collaborative inquiry on a self-selected focus of high quality learning and teaching" along with week-long summer institutes and follow-up work sessions (Partnership for Reform in Secondary Science and Mathematics, n.d.).

4) *Community partnership.* The PRiSSM project is one of several Math-Science Partnerships (MSPs) in Washington State. Another state-wide MSP project, currently in the proposal stage, is to be hosted by the University of Washington as the lead institution and will implement a unique model developed by the Mathematics Education Collaborative (MEC 2008). "The MEC Community Engagement Model actively involves the whole community, by uniting educators, families and community members in support of quality mathematics in schools. A well-informed community recognizes the value of providing appropriate learning experiences for all students and teachers; ensures that districts maintain a continuing focus on improving mathematics teaching and learning; supports and advocates for appropriate inno-

vation in mathematics education." This MSP intends to bring together mathematics and education professors from institutions of higher education, math coordinators from Educational Service Districts, administrators and support staff in school districts, school principals, teachers, parents, and community leaders—all engaged in learning more mathematics as individuals and working together. The long-range goals are to better understand how mathematics is most effectively and appropriately taught K–20, including teacher educators, mathematicians, engineers, and other professionals; and to demonstrate how school and community leaders can support high-quality mathematics instruction. The comprehensive and coordinated MEC model may serve as a prototype for large-scale, state-wide intervention and improvement in mathematics learning and teaching.

These efforts have been well publicized. However, it is not clear that they have been fully coordinated or that the various project directors have been brought together to consider how all of this work might advance reform efforts.

Washington Learns

Ten years after reform legislation passed in Washington, there were some improvements in mathematics performance but not nearly enough to meet the high expectations envisioned by the reformers, who were troubled by the mediocre improvement in scores, particularly among challenging student populations. In response, after an 18-month study, the governor's office released its November 2006 report, *Washington Learns: World-Class, Learner-Focused, Seamless Education*, which concluded that "Education is the single most important investment we can make for our children, our state, our economy and our future." The report stated further that "We propose a bold plan to redesign and re-invest in education during the next decade. We offer a new way of thinking about the purpose and function of public education, and we believe that math and science education must be addressed first." Among other methods to accomplish the bold goal of developing a world-class education system, "We will hold our students to math and science standards that match or exceed the standard of other states and nations, and we will make sure that students, from kindergarten through graduate schools, are prepared for their next level of classes" (*Washington Learns* 2006, p. 6).

Describing "Five Initiatives for a World-Class Education System" (p. 18), one of which is "Math and Science: A Competitive Edge" (p. 24), the report declares "If Washington is going to compete in the global economy . . . we all have a responsibility to get past the perception that math and science are too hard and show students that math and science are fun, interesting and that they are good at it." To realize these worthy objectives, seven strategies were proposed (pp. 24–28):

1. Develop math and science materials to train child care and early education teachers.
2. Bring world-class math and science into our classrooms.
3. Build expertise in math and science teaching.
4. Attract more math and science teachers.
5. Get students excited about math and science, using public-private partnerships.
6. Expand incentives and opportunities for students seeking high demand math- and science-related certificates and degrees.
7. Partner with after-school programs to support math learning.

In contrast to the reform goals, these strategies are focused more on developing competent math instruction and helping teachers develop the math knowledge they need for instruction. The goals are laudable as correctives to a system that has, in large part, left teachers out of the reform effort. It remains to be seen how the new strategies will create *and sustain* improved math instruction through institutional supports as well as encouragement of individual teachers.

Following the proposals and plans in the *Washington Learns* report, a news release from the Office of the Governor, dated May 21, 2007, stated: "Governor Christine Gregoire today signed an executive order that creates a council to hold state government accountable and measure progress . . . toward long-term goals for a world-class education system, established by the *Washington Learns* committee . . . The P-20 Council will be responsible for driving progress toward the ten-year goals proposed by *Washington Learns* in November 2006. The council must also improve student success and transitions within and among the early learning, K–12 and higher education sectors and, beginning in 2008, issue an annual report to Washingtonians, Governor Gregoire and the Legislature" (News release, http://www.governor.wa.gov/, accessed April 1, 2008).

It is apparent that the *Washington Learns* report, recommendations, and "assignments" have provided significant guidance for OSPI activities regarding the improvement of mathematics education in Washington. The revision of the Washington State Mathematics Standards is in its final stages, and processes are underway to select curriculum materials for districts to adopt and to plan large-scale professional development for teachers.

Math Standards in Washington State

To put in motion the recommendations in the *Washington Learns* report, it was deemed necessary to update and upgrade the student learning standards. In a draft document (Plattner 2007) titled "Washington State Mathematics Standards: Review and Recommendations," Plattner wrote that "The bottom line is that Washington's math standards need to be strengthened. If mathematics is the gateway to student success in higher education and the workplace, Washington is getting too few of its students to and through the door." She adds, however, that "Washington is moving in the right direction. The number of students passing the state's tests in math has increased. About 61 percent of the students who took the Washington Assessment of Student Learning (WASL) in June 2007 have now passed" (pp. 2–3). Comparing Washington standards with those in California, Massachusetts, and Indiana, as well as with the Singapore Curriculum, Finland Standards, NCTM Curriculum Focal Points, NAEP, the American Diploma Project, and the Washington College Readiness Mathematics Test, a panel of experts offered the following recommendations (Plattner 2007), which are representative of the kinds of recommendations now being proposed in other U.S. jurisdictions as well:

1. Set higher expectations for Washington's students by fortifying content and increasing rigor.
2. Prioritize topics to identify those that should be taught for extended periods at each grade level.
3. Place more emphasis on mathematical content and standard algorithms.
4. Write Essential Academic Learning Requirements (EALRs) that clarify grade level priorities and reflect both the conceptual and procedural sides of mathematics.

5. Increase the clarity, specificity and measurability of the Grade Level Expectations (GLEs).
6. Create a standards document that is easily used by most people.
7. Include a mathematician, a curriculum specialist and an effective teacher on the Office of Superintendent of Public Instruction (OSPI) Standards Revision Team.

These statements make concessions to both traditionalists and constructivists. To fortify content could imply teaching good problem-solving skills; putting more emphasis on content could imply either more drill or more wrestling with problems; using standard algorithms is the mantra of traditionalism. However, the effective teacher who helps guide this process of writing standards is only one voice among many in a large team of administrators and specialists in testing, advanced math, and curriculum design. The teacher's role here is a small one, and any attention paid to the special knowledge of good math teachers is minimal.[2]

In February 2007, Washington's governor and the State Superintendent of Public Instruction proposed maintaining the current math standard for graduation for the Class of 2008, rather than requiring students to pass the 10th grade WASL. A news report quotes the Superintendent of Public Instruction as saying that "Students that do not meet the [WASL] standard by the end of their junior year will qualify for a diploma by continuing to take rigorous coursework in mathematics until they graduate or pass the test." Reformers were quick to respond, saying that the WASL standard is considered a minimum threshold that all students need to meet. "The reality

---

2. The revision of the new standards for math in Washington was to be completed by Summer 2008. Information about this project can be found at http://www.sbe.wa.gov/mathstandards.htm. The web site for the Office of the Superintendent for Public Instruction is http://www.k12.wa.us/.

is that students need even higher levels of preparation in key 'gatekeeper' classes such as Algebra II to be ready for college and the world of work. . . . At the same time we must upgrade our course credit requirements for graduation. . . . Currently, Washington only requires that students take two years of unspecified math" (Partnership for Learning 2007).

Continuing the departure from using the WASL as the graduation standard, in May 2007 the Governor signed into law a measure that extends to 2013 the date by which students must meet the state math and science standards for high school graduation. Students must meet requirements through the WASL or "an alternative assessment," and students who do not meet the standard are required to take more math credits. The governor explained, "We must improve math and science teaching and learning, but we cannot penalize students when the system has failed them." (Office of the Governor 2008).

This examination of Washington State mathematics education reveals the shifting nature of the overall goals that will affect math testing, curriculum and textbook choices, continuing professional education for teachers, and classroom practice. Washington State's current mathematics program is decentralized. Individual schools and districts choose texts and materials, and a student who moves from one school or district to another may encounter a completely different curriculum and method of teaching. In the summer of 2008, OSPI was to introduce a new set of standards. This may help to unify the curriculum, but will it assist teachers in developing the specific knowledge they need for improving math instruction? Plans for teacher in-service education are in flux, without any program in place that would offer comprehensive education for teachers in profound mathematics, the design of the curriculum, or the best ways to communicate mathematical ideas to students.

The Washington School Research Center Findings

The Washington School Research Center (WSRC) at Seattle Pacific University has been evaluating educational progress in Washington State for many years. WSRC staff members have also carried out evaluation projects across the country to support their understanding of the current state of math education. When the WSRC turned its attention to mathematics education in particular, researchers examined both the reform-based/constructivist and traditionalist positions on the math wars. The preceding chapters of this book have highlighted a "middle ground" of sorts that WSRC researchers feel characterizes the approach to math education taught at the Freudenthal Institute at the University of Utrecht. In particular, this approach represents a way of teaching math that combines elements of the traditionalist and constructivist positions, which in fact is also what the U.S. National Research Council advocates.

WSRC technical studies have reached several conclusions relevant to the discussion of math education. First, low income explains a much larger percentage of variance in academic achievement than ethnicity or other factors for which data are available. Second, academic achievement is positively correlated with the amount of time spent on homework and the number of student activities a student participates in, and achievement is negatively correlated with time spent watching television. Abbott et al. (2002) found that constructivist teaching had a meaningful impact on student achievement, particularly in mathematics, where constructivism was defined as teaching that actively engages students in the curriculum. A second study of teaching methods (Abbott and Fouts 2003) also indicated that constructivist teaching methods led to higher student achievement.

These observational studies of constructivist teaching, while based on a well-tested instrument, do not necessarily show that the classrooms studied were characterized by the kind of teaching that Ma has in mind, i.e., teaching that is characterized by profound understanding of fundamental mathematics, the curriculum, and the needs of students. Overall, the observational protocols used in these studies demonstrated differences between highly traditionalist teaching methods and teaching that works to engage students in problem solving and discovery.

Perhaps the most important finding has been that if students do not understand math by the fourth grade, they are less likely to improve later, given the existing system of teaching and learning. The WSRC report (Fouts, April 2002) titled "The Power of Early Success: A Longitudinal Study of Student Performance on the WASL, 1998–2001," found that scores on the state test in 4th grade were strongly determinative for 10th grade scores. There was a lower probability that if student started out with poor scores he or she would improve enough to pass the test in high school. The study showed no difference between genders or among students of different ethnic backgrounds. The study also concluded that students who did well in the 7th grade were "more likely to have a computer at home, to feel safer at school, to spend substantially more time doing homework, to spend substantially less time watching TV and to have more ambitious plans for further education" (p. 15).

This study was replicated in 2005 (Peterson and Abbott, "The Power of Early Success 1998–2004"). The second study identified some additional factors that affect achievement, though the general findings were the same. Students who did poorly on 4th grade tests were unlikely to pass 10th grade tests. Factors that predicted academic success in math included a measure of socioeconomic status (the mother's education) and the amount of time spent each week doing homework. Both studies stressed that there would need to be interventions in the current educational system to capitalize on the power of early academic success.

Several of the WSRC research projects used data from classroom observation studies, such as the Teaching Attributes Observation Protocol (TAOP), to make determinations about the kinds of teaching utilized in a school in the aggregate. The TAOP and the STAR Classroom Observation Protocol, developed by The BERC Group, both assess the extent to which teachers are using "powerful teaching and learning" or reform-like teaching and learning strategies. Abbott and Fouts (2003), in a study that included more than 669 classroom observations, found that such learning strategies were employed only 17% of the time. However, this kind of teaching did correlate with higher WASL scores. In a later study of 1,400 classrooms, Brown and Fouts (2003) found that only 12% used constructivist teaching techniques. Several subsequent BERC studies have made similar conclusions about powerful teaching and learning using both the TAOP and STAR protocols (see, for example, Baker, Gratama, and Bachtler 2003).

Washington State Mathematics Achievement

Current Washington State math achievement scores are similar to those of most other states. A few states show better performance on the National Assessment of Educational Progress (NAEP), and a few states and the District of Columbia fall significantly below Washington State. Washington State has come later to the math wars between traditionalists and constructivists than other states, and Washington is distinctive in its decision to postpone implementation of graduation require-

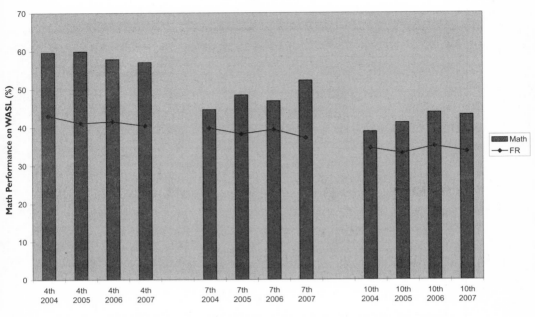

Figure 1. Math performance and family income 2004–2007

ments from 2008 to 2013 so that more time can be given to improving math instruction.

Math achievement scores of Washington schools remained fairly stable over the years 2004–2007, as shown in Figure 1.[3] While 4th grade scores on the WASL declined a bit in 2006 and 2007, 7th and 10th grade scores improved slightly or were stable from 2004 to 2007.[4] Notable in this figure is that math scores generally declined from the 4th to the 10th grades, taking all years into account.

---

3. The graph is based on data from all schools in the state of Washington in terms of % of students passing the WASL math test, and the % of students at the schools eligible for free/reduced lunch, an indicator of family income (Source: OSPI website, http://www.k12.wa.us/).

4. Changes are not statistically meaningful.

Comparing Washington and Other States

Washington's curriculum and graduation requirements can be examined from another perspective, namely, how Washington math requirements compare to those of other states. While these data are perhaps less important for understanding test results and basic student competency in math, the data do indicate a lower overall commitment to math in Washington schools that is consistent with Washington's ranking in higher education achievement.

Washington is one of 42 states that have high school graduation requirements. Washington is not one of the 20 states that require Algebra 1, or one of the 13 states that require geometry, or one of the four states that require Algebra 2 for graduation from high school. Some officials believe that it is important for students to take algebra by the end of 8th grade. Thirty-three percent of Washington students were taking algebra in 8th grade in 2005, compared to 41% across the nation. However, the push to take algebra by a particular grade is associated with the goal of taking calculus either by the end of high school or in the first year of college. As many European and American experts argue, this is not a goal that has much value when many students would be better served by learning statistics or more applied math and when colleges are well-suited to teaching calculus. As far as college admission is concerned, a further study of Washington State student transcripts indicated that students who have not completed all the required college-prep classes are most likely to have missed classes either in math or in foreign language (Stroh, et al. 2007).

The Critical Elements of Reform Efforts

In 1993, Washington reformers set out to fundamentally change the three legs of the mathematics "stool": curriculum (what was taught), instruction (the way it was taught), and assessment (the way to measure achievement). Unlike elsewhere around the country, reformers in Washington were in relative agreement on the standards, and school districts spent a decade purchasing textbooks and aligning curriculum to the new math standards. Curriculum and instruction are the "inputs" to the system, and the WASL measures the "output." Although state leadership has clearly implemented new curriculum and assessments over the last 15 years, there is little evidence of support for changes in the way the curriculum is taught or in methods to help students learn (as indicated in Figure 2 by the lack of an arrow connecting instructional input to assessment output). Fundamentally, the thing that was supposed to change after the passage of HB 1209 was classroom practice, teaching and learning. We described this dynamic earlier as second-order change. It is precisely the teaching and learning that have not changed substantially.

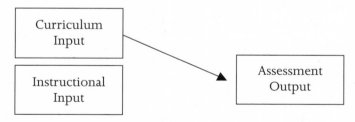

Figure 2. The three elements of the mathematics reform strategy

It is critical to recognize that mathematics reform requires a change in standards (curriculum), testing (assessments), and pedagogy (teaching and learning). Many are concerned about the outputs of the system. But what did leaders expect from over a decade of curriculum reform and testing? It could be argued that much more has been gained from the system than should have been expected, given that one of the two critical systems inputs was largely ignored. What leaders have gotten out of the last fifteen years is new curriculum aligned with new standards, tested with a new performance-based assessment, taught in the same way math has always been taught. In other words, the primary emphasis of the effort has been to change *what* we teach, not how we teach it.

For example, utilizing data from The BERC Group and Fouts & Associates, it appears that there was little change in instruction over the years of data collection, 2001–2007. This can be demonstrated by the consistency of the 2001–2007 results along with a simple comparison between the first Fouts study and the results from the 2007 BERC data collection. In 2003, Fouts collected the first state-wide data from 669 classrooms using TAOP. Since then, The BERC Group has conducted more than 10,000 classroom observations using the STAR protocol. In 2007, The BERC Group collected 1,180 classroom observations. Both Fouts and BERC use the same overall score metric. Figure 3 shows two things: 1) the majority of responses indicate that lessons were, at best, only "somewhat" aligned with reform goals, and 2) there was very little discrepancy between the two studies over several years.

How could one of the two system inputs have been overlooked? It may be due to an assumption that teachers are adaptable enough to simply conform to whatever mandate is required without attention to the necessary support. But this is shortsighted. World-class investments into how teachers approach teaching and learning are required as much as world-class investments in purchasing and aligning new curricula and standards. This is in no way to place the blame upon teachers. Changing instructional practice is a very difficult and complicated task. In order to be fully successful, it

How well was this lesson aligned with Washington State reform efforts/goals?

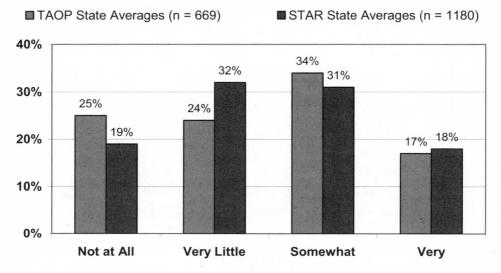

Figure 3. Classroom observation results from 2003 (TAOP) and 2007 (STAR)

has to be a system-wide effort, as we have discussed repeatedly in this book.

All three reform elements (curriculum, instruction, and assessment) need to be implemented for student achievement to match public expectations. Some Washington schools and districts have moved on without systemic (state-wide) support to try to address issues of aligning instruction; however, widespread improvement without state policy and practice that support instruction from a systemic perspective may not be likely. In general, it may be that bringing peace in the math wars is less about what curriculum teachers need to teach, or what test they need to teach to, and more about simply agreeing to see a reform effort all the way through before starting over.

It is important to recognize how the "earth shifted" with a change to standards in 1993. The standards movement changed everything about public education. This reform is intended to be about *all* students meeting standard. That means having clear standards, adequate curriculum, and reasonable assessments. But, it also means aligning the teaching and learning process so that all students can learn and achieve.

Instruction designed to sort students (as was done over a century from the 1880s to the 1980s) and instruction designed to help all students learn are two very different things. Pre-reform instruction was teacher-centered, norm-referenced, relied on compliance, and was guided by an adopted curriculum. Post-reform instruction is student-centered, criterion-referenced, relies on active inquiry, and requires the teacher to adapt the curriculum. As Schmoker (2006, p. 8) said so eloquently: "It's the Instruction, Stupid."

Why Math Reform Hasn't Worked

Over the last few years, state leaders have taken predictable steps of drafting new standards and reviewing new assessments. This continued fight over which standards and which curriculum will yield the desired outcomes may, ironically, be at the core of the problem with mathematics reform. If there is an assumption that there is something wrong only with the standards, the curriculum, or the tests, a supportive and effective system of teaching mathematics is less likely to garner the attention it deserves in the overall reform effort.

In order to move forward, state policy-makers and education practitioners need to know more about what is actually happening in classrooms statewide. This knowledge would better equip them to develop an approach to teacher education and teacher in-service education that would help create a workforce of professional math teachers with the kind of knowledge and skills imagined by Stigler, Hiebert, Ball, Ma, and others. Until that important system of continuous learning is created, perhaps with the help of the teachers themselves, state math achievement levels may continue to be simply adequate and/or similar to those of other states. Students might continue to experience a system without fundamental educational equity of opportunity and achievement, in which only some have the chance to get into highly technical careers while others are at a disadvantage from early on.

Math Teachers Left Behind

If all the reform elements are not included, state leaders will proceed with the present revisions of the math standards and assessments, perhaps adopt new standards, agree that they are good, and put in place a new assessment. In this event, what is likely is that the reform effort will not surpass the efforts of the last fifteen years.

The challenge to the state in the next round of math reform will be to prove "fidelity of the reform treatment" prior to starting over again in the next fifteen years. In typical research projects, it is crucial to determine whether a specified treatment was fully implemented before determining that the treatment did or did not work.

It may have been more productive to have spent the reform years supporting change in how to teach as much as what to teach. The current reforms seem to be headed partly in that direction, but the past does suggest the need for a continuous check on treatment fidelity. That is, a check to make sure both the curriculum and instructional inputs are supported systemically and effectively. It could be argued that the math reform of 1993 did not fail in Washington, it was just never completed. As they move forward, reformers might heed the admonition, "this time, try not to leave instruction out of the equation."

4

Conclusions and Implications

At the beginning of this volume, we identified four "critical insights" that appear to affect math education and achievement. In general terms, these stated that:

1. Reform efforts have not succeeded because teachers have not been given the support needed to teach math more effectively and to align their teaching with new standards.
2. Effective reform requires coordination among standards, assessment, and instruction. Recent reforms have focused on articulating new standards, and designing and implementing new tests, but have left instruction out.
3. High-quality curricula are necessary, but curricula alone are not sufficient to create a good math program. Teachers' knowledge of math and pedagogy is also essential.
4. Systematic and meaningful reform can occur and persist only as teachers change the view of their own work, and as educational institutions provide the resources necessary for teachers to engage in the continuous study of mathematics and the teaching of mathematics.

It is important to point out that these four fundamental insights rest on the assumption that programs to create meaningful change in math education are viewed as both "means" and "ends" to institutional change. It is often the case that school districts or department leaders identify a certain strategy purported to lead to a desired outcome, and then adopt that strategy across the board without the ownership or understanding of the individual practitioners who must "live it out." In this case, the new strategy may simply become another in a long line of "solutions" that do not result in the desired outcomes. This may partially be due to the practitioner not fully understanding or converting the strategy from a policy to a practice. Most everyone in education has experienced this dynamic.

In the WSRC publication "A Decade of Reform" (Fouts 2003), Fouts discussed the concept of first- and second-order changes in the context of educational reform efforts. He noted that change strategies

> "in and of themselves, may accomplish little because they do not *necessarily* result in a qualitatively different experience on the part of the student. What seems to happen in many schools is that so much attention and focus is placed on the outward structural, physical, or administrative changes being implemented that the underlying reasons *why* the changes are being made are ignored." (p. 12)

We might say that first-order changes are the possible means by which change can occur, not ends in themselves. Adopting a new curriculum (first-order change) may result in improved learning, but not necessarily, unless teachers and other school leaders capitalize on the specific features of the new curriculum that enable the teachers to teach better (second-order change).

Conclusions

Our findings go beyond the four insights and lead to several implications needing further consideration. We undertook this survey of the international debate in a spirit of open inquiry and without a vested interest in any of the camps that take part in the "math wars." School systems would be fortunate to avoid a repetition of those conflicts, because they polarize issues that need not be polarized, and they take time away from the work of creating a more effective system that begins with teachers—teachers who are engaged in the continuous study of math and the continuous and well-supported enhancement of their ability to reach all students.

We have noted that the international, U.S., and Washington State discussions about math are similar. Much of the concern about the failure of math education is based on comparisons among schools that are not similar, comparing elite math and science academies, for example, to average urban high schools. From the standpoint of statistically meaningful data, such as that gathered by the National Assessment of Educational Progress, Washington State is no worse off than any other state. From the perspective of the National Council of Teachers of Mathematics, the highest priority at this time is to assure educational equity. However, there does not seem to be agreement as to what students ought to learn. For example, there does not appear to be international dialogue about the specific kinds of mathematics that are most important for the emerging high-tech economy, and there is disagreement among American and European curriculum designers over the relative importance of calculus compared to statistics and applied mathematics.

Within the United States, the great debate has been between reform-based math, sometimes called constructivism, and traditionalism. It is not necessary to choose between these models, because there are curricula, such as Dutch Realistic

125

Mathematics Education, that combine aspects of both models. In fact, many practitioners of both constructivist and traditionalist teaching draw on the strengths of the other model: constructivists also teach basic skills and algorithms, and traditionalists also may call upon students to explore mathematical ideas.

We have found that the key issue in improving math education does not lie with the curriculum or with standards alone. Many teachers in the primary grades may not teach math well because they might not know much math themselves. The more creative and exploratory the curriculum, the more important it becomes for teachers to know math very well indeed. The most effective math programs in the world, such as the Japanese curriculum, combine traditional and constructivist elements and are taught by teachers who spend a great deal of time working together on lessons and talking about ways to improve teaching. Good math teaching, in fact, appears to call for a combination of abilities: an ideal math teacher knows math, studies math and math teaching continually, and is also a very good communicator. Improving math education, then, will require teachers to work collaboratively to develop these abilities.

What conclusions follow from these findings? We propose four, though the first of these is highly theoretical in nature and is less pressing.

1. Math is a dynamic discipline, and the applications of math in emerging technologies are also dynamic. The mathematics used in contemporary computer science, medical imaging, and other fields is not the same math that was critical for the industries of the 1950s. It would be interesting for a group of technological leaders to examine the domain of mathematics and

recommend a list of topics that ought to be part of a 21st century math curriculum, K–20. Even if those recommendations were not hugely different from a traditional math curriculum, it would be helpful for teachers, parents, and students to have a picture of how math applies to the full range of new careers and technological fields.

2. There is a genuine need for additional research into how students learn math, so that the best practices of master teachers can be documented and then turned into some form of training. Here in Washington State, for example, we have data on schools where students come from very poor families. And yet the students in those schools perform extraordinarily well on the state achievement test. What is it about the teachers in those schools, among other factors, that makes a difference? Is it their formal education? Is it the way they talk about and explain particular mathematical ideas? Is it the way teachers study lessons together and work to improve their presentation?

3. At the level of policy, there is a need for the state to support the educational needs of teachers. It is not enough to mandate standards and tests. Real and sustained change in math education requires that appropriate and sensitive steps be taken to help teachers become more effective in the instruction of math, with the understanding that the state's teachers have worked hard at reform and that what is proposed are measures to make time and to provide resources to improve upon work that is already being done with care and integrity.

One critical element in all of the above is support for teachers to learn the math they need in order to teach effectively. Beyond the state level, however, is the critical support available at the district level. It is here that decisions are made across schools about what curricula should be used, what the particular focus in math should be for all teachers, and what financial and time supports are available to help teachers negotiate their craft. Professional development agenda can be focused on fostering the learning of good approaches to teaching math; time can be made available for collaboration among math teachers to strengthen their understanding of specific lessons and their overall approach to teaching the material; peer observation and mentoring can be provided, especially for inexperienced teachers but also for those attempting to change their long-held approaches to teaching. These and other supports are ensured by a district administration devoted to changing the way math is taught, along with careful attention to how students best learn mathematics.

4. Interventions to help teachers more effectively and appropriately instruct *all* students require funding. Math teachers themselves could help choose or design the systems that would be used to carry out a continuous program by which they learn more math, learn more about teaching math, examine lessons, and engage in regular school-level conversations about enhancing math education. Many models for improving math education are available, but quick fixes performed by outside experts may be less effective than the ongoing work done by people who are engaged in continuous study and their own improvement. As several scholars have argued, these conversations among math teachers may be enhanced further by including teachers from

other systems or states with similar cultures, as well as teachers and professors from K–20.

To reduce it to a phrase: if we want all our children to learn math, we need our teachers to learn math more deeply themselves, and we need forward-thinking school systems to support them in the endeavor.

Large-Scale Reform

Addressing improvement of math education on a large scale may look daunting, but we are not without research to give guidance. Michael Fullan, long-time dean and now Professor Emeritus of the Ontario Institute for Studies in Education at the University of Toronto, is probably the leading researcher in the field of educational reform worldwide. Two decades ago, Fullan's studies of change efforts in schools led to his first book on the subject, entitled *Change Forces: Probing the Depths of Educational Reform* (Fullan 1993). He identified two major factors that are particularly relevant to our conclusions, which he sums up as "Reculture, not Restructure" and what he terms "Moral Purpose." From our standpoint, attempts to restructure schools and schooling are first-order changes that do not insure greater student engagement and achievement. We must, in addition, "reculture" and attend to the necessary second-order changes in individuals, in order to bring about system-wide, sustainable improvements that lead to greater student learning in mathematics. The issues related to moral purpose are playing out in classrooms and schools due to the ineffective emphasis on only two legs of the educational stool, higher standards and accountability assessments. As Fullan (2003) put it, "With all the emphasis on uninformed and informed prescription over the past twenty years, one of the casualties has been teachers' intrinsic motivation or sense of moral purpose" (p. 11). With continual, high-stakes pressure to raise test scores without support for professional learning that leads to more effective instruction, many educators struggle to keep up with all the mandates and have trouble maintaining satisfaction that they are doing a good job.

In Fullan's *The New Meaning of Educational Change: Third Edition* (Fullan 2001), he speaks to "the objective reality of educational change" describing what is involved in changing teachers' practices. Implementation of innovations in schools is "multidimensional . . . [with] at least three components or dimensions at stake: (1) the possible use of new or revised materials (instructional resources such as curriculum materials or technologies), (2) the possible use of new teaching approaches (i.e., new teaching strategies or activities), and (3) the possible alternation of beliefs (e.g., pedagogical assumptions and theories underlying particular new policies or programs)" (p. 39). According to Fullan, most educational reforms are ephemeral or shallow because they have grossly overlooked the importance of the third dimension, the alteration of beliefs. He distinguishes between change and the process of change with a 25/75 rule: educational change is 25% structural (ideas) and 75% reculturing (processes). Fullan (2008) calls for the scaling up of whole-school reform and professional learning communities, with an emphasis on shared meaning and more stakeholder transparency into each other's roles, collaboration among all groups, and school leadership, saying that "The principal is crucial to school success, and professional learning communities are more effective than individual professionals working in isolation" (p. 164).

Two examples of large-scale reform demonstrate the complexities and lessons to be learned. As described in *Education Week* (Olson 2007), leaders in Ontario, Canada, followed the results of England's national literacy and numeracy strategy, which "relied on a system of pressure and supports to improve schools." The strategy produced significant test-score gains between 1997 and 2000 but was followed by a period of leveling off. Ontario officials thought this "informed prescription" strategy dictated too much from the center and failed to adequately motivate teachers and principals. Ontario's adaptation was to staff its reform efforts by "outstanding practitioners on loan from districts" and provide adequate resources and opportunities for school improvement and teacher learning at the local level during release time and through professional development. "Staff members are expected to share their knowledge and practices through networking with other schools across the province." The result has been significant improvement by low-achieving schools, and graduation rates are up. Education officials in Ontario are quoted as saying "We've been in the boat rowing together like we've never rowed before" and "There's truly an alignment of focus and buy-in at all levels, and that's really a driving force" (Olson 2007).

A powerful study of mathematics reform in California was based on contentions by "educational reformers and policymakers that improved student learning requires stronger academic standards, stiff state tests, and school accountability" (Reische n.d.). In 2001, University of Michigan researchers Cohen and Hill published the results of their extensive study of California's decade-long campaign to improve mathematics teaching in the state's public schools (Cohen and Hill 2001). They found that "effective state reform depends on conditions that most policymakers ignore: coherent guidance for teaching and learning, and extensive opportunities for professional learning" as reported by the School of Education at the University of Michigan (Reische n.d.). Cohen and Hill examined professional education materials and surveyed nearly 600 of the state's elementary school teachers and found that the state's policy facilitated better teaching and learning only when there was consistency among tests, curricula, and classroom practice, along with ongoing opportunities for teachers to learn the practices set forth in the state's policy. When these elements were in place, teaching was congruent with the aims envisioned by the policymakers, and students' scores were higher on the state math tests. Cohen and Hill concluded that key to successful reform is the integration of policy and practice, and they suggest that American education cannot be reformed just by imposing new requirements and conducting high-stakes assessment. Teachers must have the time and opportunity to gain new knowledge and must have support for their day-to-day instruction efforts.

Scholars and policy makers referenced throughout this book have made additional recommendations and observations about large-scale change efforts, some of which we have discussed in earlier chapters. Many programs are available that can serve as models for how teachers can enhance their performance; we note in particular the recommendations of Stigler and Hiebert on "lesson study," and the intensive re-learning of mathematics of the kind offered by Parker and others through the Mathematics Education Collaborative in Washington State.

Implications

Policy solutions continue to focus on curriculum and assessment development rather than on teacher development. We conclude from our research that more effective reform policies would move beyond re-establishment of standards, re-alignment of curriculum, and re-development of assessment systems, to helping teachers know more math and know more about how to teach math effectively. Although Washington State clearly implemented new curriculum and assessments over the last 15 years, there is little evidence of support for changes in the way the curriculum is taught or of methods to help students learn.

New trends in math education may exacerbate the need to elevate the support for teachers in reform efforts. Among these trends are the following:

1. States need to be prepared for more students taking more math classes.
2. States need to be prepared for more students taking higher levels of math.
3. States will need to recruit, retain, and develop more math teachers.
4. Teachers will need support to develop a deeper knowledge of math K–12.
5. Teachers will need support to develop methods for teaching math effectively.
6. States will need to support both pre-service, alternative certification and in-service professional development in systemic ways.

Many in Washington State are currently proposing new graduation requirements that would require more math. The existing requirement is two years of math. As obvious as it may seem, it is important to point out that if graduation requirements are raised to three or even four years of math, then more students will be taking more math as a result. This means there will be a need for more math teachers and perhaps a need for fewer teachers of other subject areas. This personnel repercussion may lead many high schools to adopt different schedule configurations or to accommodate in other ways the new demand, which could distract from the necessary focus on improvement of teaching and learning.

Along with requiring more math, new policy could also

lead to higher levels of math required for graduation. If this is the case, there will be a need not only for more math teachers in general, but more higher-level math teachers capable of teaching Algebra II and trigonometry, at least; and then the need to support teacher content knowledge will be even more critical than it is already. Increasing graduation requirements to four years of math, as many are advocating, is likely to require most high schools to increase their math teaching staff by 33–50%.

Given the current shortage of math teachers, reformers must consider how to recruit, retain, and support additional math teachers. Where are the new teachers to be found? Most assume they will come from the "world of work" through alternative certification programs, rather than primarily from undergraduate schools of education. This means reformers will have to support not only in-service development of teachers already in math classrooms, but also schools of education and, particularly, alternative certification programs. If there is no more support than is currently provided, one can easily anticipate how alternative certification teachers would teach math—the same way they themselves were taught some 10, 15, or 25 years ago. In such a case, teaching effectiveness would likely not change over the next decade.

It is also important to note that support is needed for math teachers from kindergarten through high school, not just at high school levels. If reform goals are to get more students learning more mathematics, then elementary teachers will need to prepare students to take, and be successful in, higher levels of math. This could easily lead to recommendations that elementary math teachers be math-certificated in the future.

Finally, one of the most important implications for successfully improving math achievement is to provide instructional support for teachers. Research indicates that math reform efforts must include helping teachers change their practice.

Because of the difficulty of changing human practice, support for teachers would have to be clear, aggressive, and sustained over a long period of time. Teachers across the K–12 system would need help developing deeper knowledge of math, both in pre-service training and on-going during their careers.

Support for teachers, schools, and districts needs to be systemic. Putting standards and tests in place and assuming good intentions among all those in charge of implementation is not effective. Nor does leaving the focus of reform strategies to individual schools or districts likely lead to lasting change. Comprehensive reform strategies require that states create momentum and develop synergy among all educators by creating a state-wide focus on teaching and learning.

In the final analysis, the solution to the math problem in Washington State and elsewhere may rest on the very difficult work of supporting teachers one-on-one and in small groups. A model for this kind of change might be the Washington State MSP projects, where teachers join together in professional learning communities to support their change in practice.

Many teachers see this kind of collaboration to improve instruction as one of the most fundamental solutions if they are to help all students achieve in the future. In a recent study conducted by the WSRC (Baker, et al. 2008), more than 75% of the teachers surveyed indicated that their greatest need was to collaborate with their colleagues to improve instruction and align it with state reform efforts. If the very practitioners we are relying on to carry out reform in mathematics have this great an expressed need, reformers might consider longer range, more comprehensive and systemic responses than have been evident in past programs.

Bibliography

Abbott, M., D. Baker, and K. Smith. July 2007. "Lessons on Leadership: A Study of Distributed Leadership in Washington State" (Research Report No. 10). Seattle, WA: Washington School Research Center, Seattle Pacific University.

Abbott, M., and J. Fouts. February 2003. "Constructivist Teaching and Student Achievement: The Results of a School-level Classroom Observation Study in Washington" (Technical Report No. 5). Seattle, WA: Washington School Research Center, Seattle Pacific University.

Abbott, M. and J. Joireman. July 2001. "The Relationships Among Achievement, Low Income, and Ethnicity Across Six Groups of Washington State Students" (Technical Report No. 1). Seattle, WA: Washington School Research Center, Seattle Pacific University. (ERIC Document Reproduction Service No. UD034286)

Abbott, M., J. Joireman, and H. Stroh. November 2002. "The Influence of District Size, School Size and Socioeconomic Status on Student Achievement in Washington: A Replication Study Using Hierarchical Linear Modeling" (Technical Report No. 3). Seattle, WA: Washington School Research Center, Seattle Pacific University.

Advisory Committee on Mathematics Education (ACME). 2004. ACME's response to the final report of the 'Tomlinson' working group on 14–19 curriculum qualifications and reform. Retrieved February 15, 2007, from www.royalsoc.ac.uk/acme/GCSE2_press_release.html.

African Mathematical Union. 1994. AMUCHMA Newsletter 12. Retrieved February 2, 2007, from www.math.buffalo.edu/mad/AMU/amu_chma_12.html.

Agarkar, Sudhakar and S. Shirali. 2001. "Depth and Breadth in the

Mathematics Curriculum." Retrieved February 16, 2007, from www.mathforum.org/pcmi/int2001report.

Ahuja, Om P. 2006. "World-class High Quality Education for all K–12 American Students." *The Montana Mathematics Enthusiast* 3(2): 223–248.

Alberts, Bruce. 1996. Remarks by Bruce Alberts, President of the National Academy of Sciences and Chair of the National Research Council at the news conference to release the TIMSS. Retrieved February 16, 2007, from www.nationalacademies.org/onpinews/newsitem.aspx.

American Federation of Teachers (AFT). "Teaching Quality." Retrieved October 2, 2007, from http://www.aft.org/topics/teacher-quality/.

Armstrong, R. L. and D. Bitter. 2002. Review of the literature. Retrieved January 24, 2007, from www.ncacasi.org.

Atweh, Ben, Helen Forgasz, and Ben Nebres, eds. 2001. *Sociocultural Research on Mathematics Education*. London: Lawrence Erlbaum Publishers.

Auty, William. 1994. Personal communication. Corvallis, OR.

Baker, D., M. Abbott, and L. Pavese. July 2008. "On the Road to Second Order Change" (unpublished study). Seattle, WA: /Washington School Research Center, Seattle Pacific University.

Baker, D. B., C. A. Gratama, and S. D. Bachtler. 2002. *Mathematics Helping Corp: Interim Report*. Olympia, WA: Office of Superintendent of Public Instruction.

―――. 2003. *Mathematics Helping Corp: Final Report*. Olympia, WA: Office of Superintendent of Public Instruction.

Baker, D., J. Joireman, J. Clay, and M. Abbott. October 2006. "Schedule Matters: The Relationship Between Student Schedules and Performance Outcomes in Washington State High Schools" (Research Report No. 9). Seattle, WA: Washington School Research Center, Seattle Pacific University.

Ball, D. L. 1991. "Research on Teaching Mathematics: Making Subject Matter Knowledge Part of the Equation." In J. Brophy, ed., *Advances in Research on Teaching* 2:1–48. Greenwich, CT: JAI Press.

―――. 2000. "Bridging Practices: Intertwining Content and Pedagogy in Teaching and Learning to Teach." *Journal of Teacher Education* 51:241–247.

Ball, D. L., J. Ferrini-Mundy, J. Kilpatrick, R. J. Milgram, W. Schmid, and R. Schaar. 2005. "Reaching for Common Ground in K–12

Mathematics Education." American Mathematical Society, *Notices of the AMS*, October 2005, 52(9): 1055–1058.

Ball, D.L., M.H. Thames, and G. Phelps. 2007. "Content Knowledge for Teaching: What Makes It Special?" http://www-personal. umich.edu/~dball/papers/BallThamesPhelps_ContentKnowl- edgeforTeaching.pdf (accessed June 17, 2007).

BERC Group. Retrieved June 27, 2008, from http://bercgroup.com/

Best Practices in Education. 2000. Featured projects. Retrieved February 6, 2007, from web.archive.org/web/20010331194946/ www.bestpraceduc.org/.

Bjorgqvist, Ole. 2005. "Mathematics Education in Finland—What Makes It Work?" The Mathematics Education into the 21st Century Project, Universiti Teknologi Malaysia, November 25– December 1, 2005.

Blaine, Sue. 2005. "Schools to Crank Up the Maths Dial as New Curriculum Takes Over." *Business Day*. www.businessday.co.za.

Blanco, Lorenzo. 2003. "The Mathematical Education of Primary Teachers in Spain." *International Journal for Mathematics Teaching and Learning*. Retrieved February 14, 2007, from www.cimt.plymouth.ac.uk/journal/blanco1.pdf.

Boaler, Jo. 2002. *Experiencing School Mathematics*. Mahwah, NJ: Lawrence Erlbaum Associates.

Braams, Bas. 2002. "Mathematics in the OECD PISA Assessment." Retrieved February 14, 2007, from www.math.nyu.edu/mfdd/ braams/links/pisa0207.html/

Briars, Diane J. and Lauren B. Resnick. 2000. "Standards, Assessments —and What Else? The Essential Elements of Standards-based School Improvement." Center for the Study of Evaluation Technical Report 528. National Center for Research on Evaluation, Standards, and Student Testing. Graduate School of Education and Information Studies, University of California, Los Angeles.

Brown, C. and Jeffrey T. Fouts. June 2003. "Classroom Instruction in Achievers Grantee High Schools: A Baseline Report, prepared for the Bill & Melinda Gates Foundation, Washington State. Fouts & Associates, LLC. http://www.spu.edu/orgs/research/ Classroom%20Observation%20Report-Achievers%202003. pdf.

Cabrita, Isabel. September 2002. "Mathematics and Technologies: Bridging Diverse Languages." Retrieved September 7, 2007, from http://www.math.unipa.it/~grim/SiCabrita.PDF.

Caine, R. N. and G. Caine. 1991. *Making Connections: Teaching the Human Brain*. Alexandria, VA: Association for Supervision and Curriculum Development.

Campaign for Popular Education. 2000. "A Question of Quality— State of Primary Education in Bangladesh." Retrieved February 2, 2007, from www.campebd.org.

Canadian Mathematics Education Study Group. 2006. Announcement. 30th Annual Meeting, University of Calgary.

Carpenter, Thomas P., Elizabeth Fennema, Megan Loef Franke, Linda Levi, and Susan B. Empson. September 2000. "Cognitively Guided Instruction: A Research-based Teacher Professional Development Program for Elementary School Mathematics." National Center for Improving Student Learning and Achievement in Mathematics and Science (NCISLA). Retrieved October 31, 2007, from http://www.wcer.wisc.edu/ncisla/publications/reports/rr003.pdf.

Carroll, William. May 1998. "An Analysis of Everyday Mathematics in Light of the Third International Mathematics and Science Study." Available from Everyday Learning Corporation. Retrieved June 19, 2008, from http://www.edvisors.com/Detailed/Products_and_Services/Curriculum/Everyday_Learning_Corporation_30427.html.

Cavanagh, Sean. 2008a. "Panel Calls for Systematic, Basic Approach to Math." *Education Week*. Retrieved April 22, 2008, from www.edweek.org/ew/articles/2008/03/19/28math_ep.h27.html.

————. 2008b. "Catching Up on Algebra." *Education Week*. Retrieved May 7, 2008, from www. edweek.org/ew/articles/2008/04/23/34algebra_ep.h27.html.

————. 2008c. "Essential Qualities of Math Teaching Remain Unknown." *Education Week*. Retrieved April 7, 2008, from www.edweek.org/ew/articles/2008/04/02/31math.ep.h27.html.

Cech, Scott J. 2007. "2nd SAT Dip in Row Stirs Debate on 2005 Revision." *Education Week*, September 5, 2007. http://www.edweek.org/ew/articles/2007/09/05/02sat.h27.html?qs=september%205%202007%20SAT_scores.

Center for Leadership and Learning Communities. 2005. "Math Coaching in Boston." Retrieved November 1, 2007, from Cllc.edc.org/instructionalcoach05

Center for the Mathematics Education of Latinos/as. (n.d.) Bibliography "Teaching English Language Learners: Research and Practice." CEMELA website.

Center for the Study of Mathematics Curriculum (CSCM). (n.d.). Projects. Retrieved February 15, 2007, from www.dsme.msu. mathed/projects.html.

Center for Teaching Quality (CTQ). "What We Know." Retrieved October 2, 2007, from http://www.teachingquality.org/ whytqmatters/whatweknow.html

Cohen, D.K. and H.Hill, H. 2001. Learning Policy: When State Education Reform Works. New Haven, CT: Yale University Press.

Commission on Student Learning. 1994. "High Standards: Essential Learnings for Washington Students." Olympia: WA.

Connected Mathematics Project. n.d. Retrieved June 16, 2008, from http://connectedmath.msu.edu/.

Corbett, Anne. 2005. Universities and the Europe of Knowledge: Ideas, Institutions and Policy Entrepreneurship in European Union Higher Education Policy, 1955–2005. London: Macmillan Palgrave.

Davidson, David M. 1990. "An Ethnomathematics Approach to Teaching Language Minority Students." In Jon Reyhner, ed. Effective Language Education Practices and Native Language Survival, Ch. 11. Chocktaw, OK. Native American Language Issues. Retrieved January 29, 2007, from jan.ucc.nau.edu.

Davis, Michelle R. "Parents Less Worried Than Experts Over Math, Science." Education Week, September 26, 2007. http://www.edweek. org/ew/articles/2007/09/26/05stempoll.h27.html?qs=Sept ember+26,+2007+Parents_less_worried_than_experts.

Ding, Liping. 2004. "Bibliography on Chinese Research in Mathematics Education: Collaborative Group for Research in Mathematics Education." Retrieved February 13, 2007, from www. crme.soton.ac.uk/biblios/chinese_math_ed.html.

Dorji, Rinchen. 2006. "A Part-time Master of Education Program for Heads of Schools." Retrieved January 29, 2007, from www. people.stfx.ca/jgreenla/BhutanDescript2.html.

Education Connection of Texas. 1999. "School District Alert for Mathematics Textbook Selection." Retrieved April 26, 2007, from http://www.nychold.com/.

Education Week. 2007. "Teacher Quality." EPE Research Center. Retrieved October 2, 2007, from http://www.edweek.org/rc/issues/ teacher-quality/.

Eigenbrood, R. July 2004. "The Relationship Between SES and the

Multilevel Influence of School and District Size on Student Achievement: A Replication of Two Previous Studies" (Technical Report No. 7). Seattle, WA: Washington School Research Center, Seattle Pacific University.

Elkind, David. 1981. "Child Development and the Social Science Curriculum of the Elementary School." *Social Education*, October 1981, pp. 435–437.

———. 2001. *The Hurried Child*. Reading, MA: Addison-Wesley.

Ellington, Lucien. 2005. "Japanese Education."Retrieved February 16, 2007, from www.indiana.edu/~japan/digest5.html.

Ellis, Mark W. and Robert Q. Berry III. 2005. "The Paradigm Shift in Mathematics Education: Explanations and Implications of Reforming Conceptions of Teaching and Learning." *The Mathematics Educator* 5(1):7–17.

English, Lyn D., ed. 2002. *Handbook of International Research in Mathematics Education*. Mahwah, NJ: Lawrence Erlbaum.

Fagin, Barry. (n.d.). "Reforming K–12 Mathematics Education." www.nychold.com/talk-fagin-040202/pdf.

Fletcher, J. A. 2005. "Constructivism and Mathematics Education in Ghana." *Mathematics Connection*, Vol 5. 2005: 29–36. Retrieved January 29, 2007, from www.ajol,info.

Fortmann, Thomas, Arthur Eisenkraft, and Hannah Sevian. 2005. "World Class: The Massachusetts Agenda to Meet the International Challenge for Math- and Science-educated Students. Mass Insight Education and Research Institute, June 2005.

Fouts, J. April 2002. "The Power of Early Success: A Longitudinal Study of Student Performance on the Washington Assessment of Student Learning, 1998–2001" (Research Report No. 1). Seattle, WA: Washington School Research Center, Seattle Pacific University.

———. April 2003. "A Decade of Reform: A Summary of Research Findings on Classroom, School, and District Effectiveness in Washington State" (Research Report No. 3). Seattle, WA: Washington School Research Center, Seattle Pacific University. Retrieved June 27, 2008, from http://spu.edu/orgs/research/ADecadeofReformOctober192003v5.pdf.

Fouts, J., M. Abbott, and D. Baker. May 2002. "Bridging the Opportunity Gap: How Washington Elementary Schools are Meeting Achievement Standards" (Research Report No. 2). Seattle, WA: Washington School Research Center, Seattle Pacific University.

Fouts, J. and Carol S. Brown. January 2002. "Mathematics Helping Corp 2001 Final Evaluation Report," prepared for the Office of the Superintendent of Public Instruction, Washington State. Fouts & Associates, LLC. Retrieved June 27, 2008, from http://spu.edu/orgs/research/MHCFinalReport2001.pdf.

Frankenstein, Marilyn. (n.d.). "The Critical Mathematics Educators Group (CMEG): Attempting to Connect Anti-capitalist Work with Mathematics Education." Retrieved February 2, 2007, from www.nottingham.ac.uk/csme/meas/plenaries/frankenstein.html.

Fredrickson, Terry. 2002. "British Education in a Thai Environment." Bangkok post learning post. Retrieved February 9, 2007, from www.bangkok post.net/education.

Fullan, M. 1993. Change Forces: Probing the Depths of Educational Reform. London: Falmer Press.

———. 2001. The New Meaning of Educational Change, 3rd edition. New York: Teachers College Press.

———. 2003. Change Forces with a Vengeance. London: RoutledgePalmer.

———. 2008. The New Meaning of Educational Change, 4th edition. New York: Teachers College Press.

———. 2008. "School Leadership's Unfinished Agenda." Education Week, April 7, 2008. Retrieved April 22, 2008, from www.edweek.org/ew/articles/2008/04/09/32fullan.h27.html.

Garelick, Barry. 2006. "Miracle Math." Retrieved February 15, 2007, from www.hoover.org/publications/ednext/38533357.html.

Greenberg, Julie and Kate Walsh. 2008. "No Common Denominator." National Council for Teacher Quality. Retrieved July 11, 2008, from www.nctq.org.

Greene, Elizabeth. 2000. Chronicle of Higher Education.

Grouws, Douglas A. and Kristin J. Cebulla. 2001. "Improving Student Achievement in Mathematics." International Academy of Education, UNESCO. Lausanne, Switzerland.

Hall, Daria and Shana Kennedy. 2006. Primary Progress, Secondary Challenge: A State-by-State Look at Student Achievement Patterns. The Education Trust, March 2006. http://www2.edtrust.org/NR/rdonlyres/15B22876-20C8-47B8-9AF4-FAB148A225AC/0/PPSCreport.pdf.

Hanlon, Ginger. 1998. "Dutch Constructivist Methods in Elementary School Mathematics." Retrieved February 6, 2007, from web.archive.org/web19981202015209/www.bestpraceduc.org/DiscoveryGrants1996/.

Harper, James. 2001. "Mathematics Education Dialogues: Some Thoughts on Why Japanese Students Are Better than US Students on International Mathematics Assessments. Retrieved February 16, 2007, from www. nctm.org/dialogues/2001-11/20011107.html.

Hiebert, James. (n.d.) "What Research Says about the NCTM Standards," in "High School Physics Enrollment Hits Record High." *Science Daily.* Retrieved April 26, 2007, from www.sciencedaily.com.

Hill, H. C., and D. L. Ball. 2004. "Learning Mathematics for Teaching: Results from California's Mathematics Professional Development Institutes." *Journal for Research in Mathematics Education,* 35 (5): 330–351.

Hill, H. C., B. Rowan, and D. Ball. 2005. "Effects of Teachers' Mathematical Knowledge for Teaching on Student Achievement." *American Educational Research Journal,* 42(2):371–406.

Holmes Group. 1986. *Tomorrow's Teachers.* East Lansing, MI: The Holmes Group, Inc.

Howson, Geoffrey. "The Value of Comparative Studies," cited in G. Kaiser, E. Luna, and I. Huntley, eds., *International Comparisons in Mathematics Eductation,* pp. 165–188. London: Falmer Press.

Hyerle, D. 1996. *Visual Tools for Constructing Knowledge.* Alexandria, VA: Association for Supervision and Curriculum Development.

Ingersoll, R. June 1998. "The Problem of Out-of-Field Teaching." Retrieved October 2, 2007, from http://www.pdkintl.org/kappan/king9806.html.

International Association for the Evaluation of Educational Achievement (n.d.). "Brief History of the IEA." Retrieved February 21, 2007, from www.iea.nl/brief_history_of_iea.98.html.

International Journal for Mathematics Teaching and Learning. Bibliography. Retrieved February 12, 2007, from www.cimt.plymouth.ac.uk/journal/default.html.

Isaacs, A., W. M. Carroll, and M. Bell. 1997. "A Research-based Curriculum: The Research Foundations of the USCMP Everyday Mathematics Curriculum." Available from Everyday Learning Corporation. Retrieved June 19, 2008, from http://www.edvisors.com/Detailed/Products_and_Services/Curriculum/Everyday_Learning_Corporation_30427.html.

Joireman, J., and M. Abbott. January 2004. "Structural Equation Models Assessing Relationships Among Student Activities, Ethnicity, Poverty, Parents' Education, and Academic Achievement" (Technical Report No. 6). Seattle, WA: Washington School Research Center, Seattle Pacific University.

Kaiser, Gabriele, Eduardo Luna, and Ian Huntley, eds. 1999. "International Comparisons in Mathematics Education." *Studies in Mathematics Education*, series 11. London: Falmer Press.

Keele University. (n.d.) Cognitive Acceleration in Mathematics Education. www.keele.ac.uk/depts/ed/cpdactivities/came-docs/thinking%20about%20joining%20CAME@KEELE.pdf (accessed January 27, 2007).

Keitel, Christine and Jeremy Kilpatrick. 1999. The Rationality and Irrationality of International Comparative Studies. In Kaiser, Luna, and Huntley (1999).

Kitchen, Richard S., J. DePree, S. Celedon-Pattichis, and J. Brinkerhoff. 2007. *Mathematics Education at Highly Effective Schools that Serve the Poor: Strategies for Change.* New Jersey: Routledge.

Klein, David. 2003. "A Brief History of American K–12 Mathematics Education in the 20th Century." Retrieved July 2, 2008, from www. cnun.edu/~vmcth00m/AHistory.html.

————. 2005. "The State of State Math Standards." Thomas B. Fordham Foundation, January 2005. http://www.edexcellence. net/issues/results.cfm?withall=the+state+of+state+math+standards+2005&search_btn.x=21&search_btn.y=10.

Kloosterman, Peter, and Frank K. Lester, eds. 2007. "Results and Interpretations of the 2003 Mathematics Assessment of the National Assessment of Education Progress. Reston, VA: The National Council of Teachers of Mathematics.

Koblitz, N. 1996. "The Case Against Computers in K–13 Math Education (Kindergarten through Calculus)." Retrieved February 5, 2007, from www. math.washington.edu/koblitz/mi.html.

Krainer, Konrad. (n.d.) "Theory and Practice: Facilitating Teachers' Investigation into Their Own Teaching: Reflection on Barbara's Teaching Experiment." European   Research in Mathematics Education III. Retrieved from Konrad. Krainer@uni-klu.ac.at.

Lam, Louisa. (n.d.). "Mathematics Education Reform in Hong Kong." Retrieved January 29, 2007, from www. math,unipa.it~grim/SiLamPDF

Learning Technologies and Mathematics Middle East Conference,

Sultan Qaboos University, Muscat, Oman. 2007. Retrieved February 2, 2007, from www.math.arizona.edu.

Loveless, Tom. 2006. *The 2006 Brown Center Report on American Education: How Well Are American Students Learning?* Washington DC: The Brookings Institution. Retrieved February 6, 2007, from http://www.brookings.edu/gs/brown/bc_report/2006/2006report.pdf.

Luitel, Bal Chandra and P. C. Taylor (n.d, under review.) "Envisioning Transition toward Transformative Mathematics Education: A Nepali Educator's Autoethnographic Perspective." In J. Earnest and D. Treagust, eds., *Educational Change and Reconstruction in Societies in Transition: International Perspectives.* Perth: Black Swan.

Ma, Liping. 1999. *Knowing and Teaching Elementary Mathematics: Teachers' Understanding of Fundamental Mathematics in China and the United States.* Mahwah, NJ: Lawrence Erlbaum Associates.

Macnab, Donald S. 2000. "Forces for Change in Mathematics Education: The Case of TIMMS." *Education Policy Analysis Archives* 8(15): 1–18.

Mallinson, Philip. Personal communication, Seattle, WA, July 18, 2007.

Martin, B. and B. Crowell. 2000. "Historical Change: Missouri Moves into the Millenium." *The Delta Kappa Gamma Bulletin* 66 (2):50–56.

Mass Insight Education and Research Institute. April 2004. "More Math, Please: The Surprising Consensus on Math among Parents, the Public, and Business Leaders in Two 'New Economy' States." Retrieved February 6, 2007, from http://www.massinsight.org/docs/MoreMathPlease.pdf.

———. May 2004. "Lessons from the Front Lines of Standards-based Reform: Four Benchmarks for an Effective State Program." Retrieved February 7, 2007, from http://www.massinsight.org/docs/Lessons-Learned.pdf.

Math Solutions Professional Development. 2008. "Five-Day Courses." http://www.mathsolutions.com/index.cfm?page=wp8&crid=15.

McDuffie, Amy Roth. 2004. "Mathematics Teaching as a Deliberate Practice: An Investigation of Elementary Pre-service Teachers; Reflective Thinking During Student Teaching." *Journal of Mathematics Teacher Education* 7(1):33–61. Retrieved March 10, 2008, from http://education.wsu.edu/directory/faculty/rothmcduffiea/.

———. 2005. "The Teacher as Researcher." In K. Appleton, ed., *Elementary Science Teacher Education: Contemporary Issues and Practices.* Hillsdale, NJ: Lawrence Erlbaum Associates. Retrieved March 10, 2008, from http://education.wsu.edu/directory/faculty/rothmcduffiea/.

McNaught, Melissa and Seoung Joun Won. October 2006. "The Consistency of Views and Practices of U.S. and South Korean Mathematics." Retrieved January 24, 2007, from www. iea. nl/fileadministrator/user_upload/IRC2006/IEA_Program/TIMSS/Mcnaught_Won.pdf.

Memorandum to Presidential Commission of Enquiry into Education. [Zimbabwe]. Retrieved February 5, 2007, from www. uz.ac.zw/science/maths/zimahs/41/edcomm.html.

Mina, Fayez and Alan Rogerson. 2007. "Mathematics Education into the 21st Century Project." *Proceedings of Conferences of 21st Century Project.* Retrieved February 6, 2007, from www.math.unipa.it/~grim/21project.html.

Monk, D. H. 1994. "Subject Matter Preparation of Secondary Mathematics and Science Teachers and Student Achievement." *Economics of Education Review* 13(2):125–145.

Monteiro, C. E. F. and M. M. F. Pinto. (n.d.) "Challenges Facing the Teaching of Mathematics Student Teachers." Retrieved January 28, 2007, from www.weizmann.ac.il/G-math/ICMI/Pinto_Marcia_ICMI_prop.doc.

National Assessment of Educational Progress. "NAEP: The Nation's Report Card." (n.d.) Retrieved September 20, 2007, from http://nationsreportcard.gov/about_nrc.asp.

National Center for Education Statistics. 1999. "Education Indicators: An International Perspective." Retrieved February 2, 2007, from neces.ed.gov/surveys/international/intlindicators/index.asp.

———. January 1999. "Teacher Quality: A Report on the Preparation and Qualifications of Public School Teachers." Retrieved October 2, 2007, from http://nces.ed.gov/surveys/frss/publications/1999080/index.asp.

———. (n.d.) "What is TIMMS?" Retrieved September 19, 2007, from http://nces.ed.gov/timss/faq.asp.

National Commission on Excellence in Education. 1983. *A Nation at Risk: The Imperative for Educational Reform.* Washington, DC: Government Printing Office. http://www.ed.gov/pubs/NatAtRisk/risk.html.

National Commission on Teaching and America's Future. 1997. *Doing What Matters Most: Investing in Quality Teaching.* New York: NCTAF.

National Council of Teachers of Mathematics. 1980. *An Agenda for Action.* Reston, VA: NCTM.

———. 1989. *Curriculum and Evaluation Standards for School Mathematics.* Reston: VA: NCTM.

———. 1991. *Professional Standards for Teaching Mathematics.* Reston, VA: NCTM.

———. 1995. *Assessment Standards for School Mathematics.* Reston, VA: NCTM.

———. 2000. *Principles and Standards for School Mathematics.* Reston, VA: NCTM.

———. 2003. *A Research Companion to Principles and Standards for School Mathematics.* Reston, VA: NCTM.

———. 2005. *Standards and Curriculum: A View from the Nation.* Reston, VA: NCTM.

———. 2006. *Curriculum Focal Points for Prekindergarten through Grade 8 Mathematics: A Quest for Coherence.* Reston, VA: NCTM.

National Mathematics Advisory Panel. 2008. "Foundations for Success: The Final Report of the National Mathematics Advisory Panel." Washington, DC: U.S. Department of Education.

National Research Council. 1999. *Teaching, Testing, and Learning: A Guide for States and School Districts.* R. F. Elmore and R. Rothman, eds.. Washington, DC: National Academy Press. Retrieved July 10, 2007, from http://books.nap.edu/catalog/9609.html.

———. 1999a. *How People Learn: Brain, Mind, Experience, and School.* Committee on Developments in the Science of Learning. J. D. Bransford, A. L. Brown, and R. R. Cocking, eds. Commission on Behavioral and Social Sciences and Education. Washington, DC: National Academy Press.

———. 1999b. *How People Learn: Bridging Research and Practice.* Committee on Developments in the Science of Learning. M. S. Donnovan, J. D. Bransford, and W. Pellegrino, eds. Commission on Behavioral and Social Sciences and Education. Washington, DC: National Academy Press.

———. 2001. *Adding It Up: Helping Children Learn Mathematics.* J. Kilpatrick, J. Swafford, and B. Findell, eds. Mathematics Learning Study Committee, Center for Education, Division of Behavioral and Social Sciences and Education. Washington, DC: National Academy Press.

Newmann, F. M. and G. G. Wehlage. 1993. "Standards of Authentic Instruction." *Educational Leadership*, 50(7):8–12.

Nicholas Bourbaki. (n.d.) Retrieved February 5, 2007, from en.wikipedia.org/wiki/Bourbaki.

North Central Regional Educational Laboratory. (n.d.) "Constructivist Teaching and Learning Models." Retrieved January 29, 2007, from www. ncrel.org/sdrs/areas/issues.

NYC HOLD. 2007. "A Quality Math Curriculum in Support of Effective Teaching for Elementary Schools," published January 3, 2007, by Educational Studies in Mathematics, retrieved September 26, 2007, from http://www.nychold.com/.

Ocken, Stanley. 2007. "Reflections on the NCTM Focal Points." Retrieved April 26, 2007, from www. nychold.com.

Office of the Governor, State of Washington. News release. Retrieved April 14, 2008, from http://www.governor.wa.gov/news/news-view.asp.

Olson, Lynn. 2007. "Ontario Pins Hopes on Practices, Not Testing, to Achieve." *Education Week*, October 24. Retrieved January 3, 2008, from www. edweek.org/ew/articles/2007/10/24/09ontario.h27.

Orey, D. C. and K. T. Nguyen. (n.d.). Working title: "The Ethnomathematics of Vietnamese Algorithms." Retrieved January 29, 2007, from www.csus.edu/indiv/o/oryd.

Orey, Daniel Clark and Milton Rosa. 2006. "Ethnomathematics: Cultural Assertions and Challenges toward Pedagogical Action." *The Journal of Mathematics and Culture* 1(1).

Partnership for Learning. February 2007. News release. Retrieved February 12, 2007, from http://www.partnership4learning.org/eBriefing/matheview/.

Penjore, Ugyen. 2007. "New Mathematics Textbooks." Kuensel online: Bhutan's daily news site. January 29, 2007.

Peterson, K., and M. Abbott. July 2005. "The Power of Early Success 1998–2004: A Follow-Up Study on the Determinants of Student Performance" (Research Report No. 8). Seattle, WA: Washington School Research Center, Seattle Pacific University.

Plattner, Linda. July 2007. *Report: Washington State Mathematics Standards Review and Recommendations*. Millersville, MD: Strategic Teaching. www. strategicteaching.com.

Raimi, Ralph. 2006. "Recent Events in French Education." Retrieved

February 16, 2007, from www.math.rochester.edu/people/faculty/rarm/slecc9.html.

RAND Mathematics Study Panel, Deborah L. Ball, chair. 2003. "Mathematical Proficiency for All Students: Toward a Strategic Research and Development Program in Mathematics Education." RAND Education.

Ravitch, Diane. 2005. "Ethnomathematics: Even Math Education Is Being Politicized." *Wall Street Journal Opinion Journal.* Retrieved January 29, 2007, from www.opinionjournal.com/extra/?id=110006873.

Reasoning Mind. (n.d.). "Highlights of the RM Methodology in Math Education." Retrieved February 7, 2007, from www. reasoningmind.org/philosophy/highlights.php3.

Reische, Jim. (n.d.) School of Education, University of Michigan Research and Outreach. Retrieved May 19, 2008, from http://www.soe.umich.edu/adifference/cohenhill/index.html.

Reys, Robert. 2002. "Reform Math Education." *Christian Science Monitor*, November 15, 2002. Retrieved October 23, 2007, from http://mathematicallysane.com/analysis/mathedreform.asp/.

Rho, Jane. (n.d.). "Korean versus American Elementary Education." Retrieved February 15, 2007, from www.sitemaker.umich.edu/rho.356/mathematics_curriculum.

Rice, Jennifer King. 2003. *Teacher Quality: Understanding the Effectiveness of Teacher Attributes.* Washington, D.C.: Economic Policy Institute.

Richardson, Kathy. July 3, 2008. Personal communication.

Riordan, Julie E. and P. E. Noyce. 2001. "The Impact of Two Standards-based Mathematics Curricula on Student Achievement in Massachusetts." *Journal for Research in Mathematics Education* 32(4): 368–398.

Rosen, L. 2000. "Calculating Concerns: The Politics of Representation in California's "Math Wars." Unpublished doctoral dissertation. University of California, San Diego. [Quoted in Schoenfeld, 2004]

Rotberg, Iris. (n.d.). "How We Measure Up: Is American Math and Science Education in Decline?" *New Atlantis.* Retrieved February 12, 2007, from www.thenewatlantis.com/archive/9/soa/education.html.

———. 1998. "Interpretation of International Test Score Comparisons." *Science*, May 15, 1998, 280:1030–1031.

Schmoker, Mike. 2006. *Results Now: How We Can Achieve Unprecedented Improvements in Teaching and Learning.* Alexandria, VA: Association for Supervision and Curriculum Development.

Schoenfeld, A. H. 2002. "Making Mathematics Work for All Children: Issues of Standards, Testing and Equity." *Educational Researcher* 31 (1):13–25.

Schoenfeld, Alan H. 2004. "The Math Wars." *Educational Policy* 18 (1): 253–286.

Sfard, Anna. 2003. "Balancing the Unbalanceable: The NCTM Standards in Light of Theories of Learning Mathematics," in *A Research Companion to Principles and Standards for School Mathematics.* Reston, VA: National Council of Teachers of Mathematics.

Shanghai Jiao Tong University. (n.d.) "World's Top Universities." Retrieved from www.ed.sjtu.edu.cn/rank.

Silicon Valley Mathematics Initiative. 2006. "Pedagogical Content Coaching." Retrieved November 1, 2007, from http://www.noycefdn.org/math/documents/PedagogicalContentCoaching.pdf.

Smaller Learning Communities 2006 Leadership Institute. "What Is a Mathematics Coach or Mentor?" Retrieved November 1, 2007, from http://www.nwrel.org/scpd/sslc/institutes_2007/documents/forum_2/chase/mathematics_coach.pdf.

Smith, Karen C. 1993. *Developmentally Appropriate Practices in Mathematics.* Portland, OR: The Oregon Mathematics Teacher.

Staats-Usher, Lisa. Los Angeles County Office of Education, Downey, CA. Interview, August 2007.

Stanic, G. M.A. 1987. "Mathematics Education in the United States at the Beginning of the Twentieth Century." In Thomas S. Popkewitz, ed., *The Formation of School Subjects: The Struggle for Creating an American Institution,* pp. 147–183. New York: Falmer.

Starr, Linda. 2005. "Math Education in the US, Germany, and Japan: What Can We Learn from This?" Retrieved January 25, 2007, from www.educationworld.com.

Stehlikova, Nada and Hejny, Milan. 1999. "The Teacher—The Decisive Agent in the Quality of Teaching." Retrieved April 17, 2007, from userweb.pedf.cuni.cz/kmdm/katedra/prednasky/09.html.

Stevenson, H. W. and J. Stigler. 1992. "Why Our Schools are Failing and What We Can Learn from Japanese and Chinese Education." *The Learning Gap.* New York: Summit Books.

Stigler, James and James Hiebert. 1997. "Understanding and Improving Classroom Mathematics Instruction: An Overview of the TIMSS Video Study." *Phi Delta Kappan*, vol. 78, p. 1.

————. 1999. *The Teaching Gap: Best Ideas from the World's Teachers for Improving Education in the Classroom.* New York: The Free Press.

Stroh, H., Jeffrey T. Fouts, and Candace C. Gratama. May 2007. "Washington State High School Graduates' College Elligibility, College Attendance, and Persistence Rates: Graduating Classes of 2004 and 2005," prepared for the Bill & Melinda Gates Foundation, Seattle, WA. Fouts & Associates, LLC. http://www.spu.edu/orgs/research/WA%20Transcripts%20and%20NSC%20report%204-02-07%20with%20appendices%20FINAL.pdf.

Sutherland, P. 1992. *Cognitive Development Today: Piaget and His Critics.* London: Paul Chapman Publishing Ltd.

Third International Math and Science Study. 2003. "Results. National Center for Education Statistics (IES)." Retrieved September 25, 2007, from http://nces.ed.gov/timss/results03.asp.

———— 2003. "Tables. National Center for Education Statistics (IES)." Retrieved January 5, 2007, from www. nces.ed.gov/timss/TIMSS03Tables.asp.

Treisman, Phillip Michael (Uri). 1985. "A Study of the Mathematical Performance of Black Students at the University of California, Berkeley." Dissertation, University of California, Berkeley.

Treisman, Uri. 1992. "Studying Students Studying Calculus: A Look at the Lives of Minority Mathematics Students in College." *College Mathematics Journal* 23(5):362–372.

Uddin, Mohsin. (n.d.). "Numeracy in Bangladesh: Terminal Competencies of Mathematics at Primary Education." Hiroshima University Graduate School for International Development and Cooperation.

U.S. Department of Education. National Center for Education Statistics. 1996b. "Out-of-field Teaching and Educational Equality." Statistical Analysis Report No. 96-040, by Richard M. Ingersoll. Washington, DC: U.S. Government Printing Office.

University of Wisconsin, Milwaukee, School of Education: Center for Mathematics and Science Education Research. "Content-focused Coaching and Leadership: Developing School Teams as Professional Learning Communities for Mathematics." Retrieved November 1, 2007, from http://www.soe.uwm.edu/pages/welcome/Centers/Center_for_Mathematics_Science_Ed.pdf.

Van de Walle, John A. 1999. Presentation for the 77th Annual Meeting of NCTM on April 23, 1999. "Reform Mathematics vs. The Basics: Understanding and Conflict and Dealing with It." Retrieved October 23, 2007, from http://www.mathematically-sane.com/.

———. 2007. *Elementary and Middle School Mathematics: Teaching Developmentally*, 6th ed. Boston: Pearson Education, Inc.

Van den Heuvel-Panhuizen, M. 2000. "Mathematics Education in the Netherlands: A Guided Tour." Freudenthal Institute CD-Rom for ICEM0. Utrecht: Utrecht University.

Vasco, Carlos E. 1999. "A Brief Report on the Tenth Inter-American Conference on Mathematics Education." The International Commission on Mathematics Instruction (ICMI), Bulletin No. 47.

Vergano, D. 1996. "Science and Math Education: No Easy Answer." *Science News*, November 30, 1996, 15(22):341.

Warfield, Virginia. April/May 2007. "New Math vs. Reform Math." *Newsletter of the Association for Women in Mathematics*. Retrieved October 31, 2007, from http://www.math.washington.edu/~warfield/news/news139.html.

———. September 18 2007. Personal communication, Seattle, WA.

Washington Association of Colleges for Teacher Education (WACTE). November 2006. "Improving Success in Mathematics: Research and Projects Underway in the State of Washington." Retrieved March 7, 2008, from www.wacte.org/mathmethods.

Washington Learns: World-Class, Learner-Focused, Seamless Education. November 2006. Retrieved March 10, 2008, from http://www.washingtonlearns.wa.gov/report/FinalReport.pdf.

"Washington State Mathematics Standards." Retrieved April 1, 2008, from http://www.utdanacenter.org/wamathrevision/standards.php.

West Ed: Schools Moving Up. "Math Matters." Retrieved November 1, 2007, from http://www.wested.org/pub/docs/625.

Widjaja, Yenni. 2004. "An MBL Mathematics Project in Indonesia." Retrieved January 25, 2007, from www.science.uva.nl/research/amstel/masters/index.

Wilson, B., M. Abbott, J. Joireman, and H. Stroh. November, 2002. "The Relations Among School Environment Variables and Student Achievement: A Structural Equation Modeling Approach to Effective Schools Research" (Technical Report No. 4). Seattle, WA: Washington School Research Center, Seattle Pacific University.

"World Mathematical Year 2000." Retrieved January 25, 2007, from www.wmy2000.math.jussieu.fr.

Wu, Hung-Hsi. 1999. "Basic Skills versus Conceptual Understanding: A Bogus Dichotomy in Mathematics Education." *American Educator*, journal of the American Federation of Teachers, Fall 1999.

Zanzali, Noor Azlan Ahmad. 2003. "Implementing the Intended Mathematics Curriculum: Teachers' Beliefs about the Meaning and Relevance of Problem Solving" Proceedings of the International Conference, The Decidable and the Undecidable in Mathematics Education. Brno, Czech Republic. September 2003.

Zulkardi. (n.d.) "How to Design Mathematics Lessons Based on the Realistic Approach." Retrieved January 25, 2007, from www.geocities.com/ratuilma/rme.html.

Zulkardi, N. Nieveen, J. Van den Akker, and J. De Lange. (n.d.) "Implementing a 'European' Approach to Mathematics Education in Indonesia through Teacher Education."

Additional Websites

"Comparison of Hong Kong and United States Schools." Retrieved February 16, 2007, from sitemaker.umich.edu/li356/math_education.

"Constructivism in the Classroom. Mathematics Education." Retrieved January 29, 2007, from www. mathforum.org/mathed/constructivism.html.

Curriculum Review: Singapore Math Grades 1–3. Retrieved February 15, 2007, from www.welltrainedmind.com/J)1singapore.html.

"Ethnomathematics: An Absolutely Essential Key for Mathematics Education. 1998. Retrieved January 29, 2007, from www.dm.unipi.it/~jama/ethno/.

"Ethnomathematics—A Rich Cultural Diversity." (n.d.). *Nova: Science in the News*. Retrieved January 29, 2007, from www. science.org.au/nova/073/073key.html.

Math Perspectives Teacher Development Center. 2008. http://www.mathperspectives.com/ (accessed July 10, 2008).

Mathematically Correct website. www.mathematicallycorrect.com.

Mathematics Case Study Project. (n.d.) http://mcsp.ewu.edu/ (accessed March 10, 2008).

"Mathematics Education Bibliography." 1997. Retrieved February 2, 2007, from www. nottingham.ac.edu/csme/booklist.html.

Mathematics Education Collaborative. 2008. http://www.mec-math. org/ (accessed June 27 and July 10, 2008).

Mathematics Education in the 21st Century Project. (n.d.). http:// math.unipa.it/~grim/21project.htm (accessed June 16, 2008).

Mathematics Education Collaborative (MEC). http://www.mec-math.org/ (accessed June 27, 2008).

National Board for Professional Teaching Standards. 2008. http:// www.nbpts.org/

National Council for Accreditation of Teacher Education (NCATE). http://www.ncate.org/

Partnership for Reform in Secondary Science and Mathematics. http: www.vancouver.wsu.edu/programs/edu/prism/index.htm (accessed March 10, 2008).

Index

About the Authors

Martin Abbott, Ph.D., is the executive director of the Washington School Research Center, an independent research and data analysis center funded by the Bill & Melinda Gates Foundation, and is professor of sociology at Seattle Pacific University.

Duane Baker, Ed.D., is director of research at the WSRC and president of The BERC Group, Inc. He and his associates have done evaluation studies across the United States and have completed more than 10,000 classroom observations using the BERC-developed STAR Classroom Observation Protocol.

Karen Smith, Ed.D., is a WSRC researcher and Presidential awardee in mathematics education with broad experience as a teacher, school administrator, and math education consultant in Oregon and Washington.

Thomas Trzyna, Ph.D., is an educational consultant and co-author of *Towards a Global Ph.D.?*, a study completed by the Center for Innovation and Research in Graduate Education at the University of Washington.

All four authors are affiliated with Seattle Pacific University.